I0820166
STROT
BERT
POIDS NET
50GR.
DE SARAWAK
LE BISTROT
PAUL BERT
Paris

BISTROT PAUL BERT

A la carte

- TERRINE DE CAMPAGNE MAISON 10€
- TEMPURA DE SARDINES & SAUCE TARTARE 12€
- CARPACCIO DE BOEUF AU BASILIC 15€
- BURRATINA DES POUILLES, OLIVES NOIRES & BASILIC 18€
- OMELETTE AUX GIROLLES 18€
- CARPACCIO DE DAURADE & VINAIGRETTE AU FRUIT DE LA PASSION 18€
- SALADE DE TOMATES MULTICOLORES AU BASILIC 12€

Les viandes rouges sont servies bleues, saignantes ou mal cuites

- PAVÉ DE SAUMON FROID, TAGLIATELLES DE COURGETTES, AIL DES OURS 38€
- SOLE MEUNIÈRE DU GUILVINEC, POMMES VAPEUR 65€
- TARTARE DE BOEUF, FRITES MAISON & SALADE VERTE 26€
- ROGNON DE VEAU À LA MOUTARDE, PURÉE MAISON 32€
- CARRÉ D'AGNEAU RÔTI AU JUS, PETITS POIS, CAROTTES 44€
- FILET DE BOEUF AU POIVRE DE SARAWAK, FRITES MAISON 46€
- ALOYAU DE BOEUF SAUCE POIVRE, POMMES SAUTÉES (2 pers) 78€
- ASSIETTE DE FROMAGES DE LA MAISON BORDIER 18€
- CRÈME CARAMEL 10€
- ÎLE FLOTTANTE AUX PRALINES ROSES 10€
- TARTE FINE AUX POMMES 12€
- SOUFFLÉ GRAND MARNIER 14€
- MACARON AUX FRAISES 14€
- FRAISES "MARA des Bois" & CRÈME CRUE 15€

La maison n'accepte pas les chèques / TTC / TVA :

LE BISTROT PAUL BERT

LE BISTROT PAUL BERT

FRENCH COMFORT FOOD FROM THE PARISIAN RESTAURANT

Bertrand Auboyneau and Gwénaëlle Cadoret

with text and photographs by Annabelle Schachmes

Abrams, New York

PARIS HAS A HEART

YVES CAMDEBORDE

The "belly of Paris" defined my entire childhood. My papa worked at the food markets of Les Halles during the 1950s, and Émile Zola's remarkable novel with the title *The Ventre de Paris* (*The Belly of Paris*) captivated me with its brilliance. In his work, Zola describes Les Halles as the belly of Paris, depicting it as a vibrant character all its own. This idea is echoed in Jean Duvivier's 1956 film *Voici le temps des assassins* (*Deadlier Than the Male*), in which Jean Gabin portrays the owner of café Au Rendez-vous des Innocents. The film possesses an extraordinary sense of finesse and truth, though admittedly not as humorous as the stuffed cabbage scene in the 1968 comedy *Le Tatoué* (*The Tattooed*). Yes, Paris certainly has a belly, but where is its heartbeat?

When I arrived in Paris to work at the Ritz, I would stroll the streets soaking in the sights, smells, and sounds to get a sense of the city's rhythm. During one of my walks, I made my way up boulevard Saint-Antoine, passing by its cabinet-making workshops, to the Reuilly intersection. My curiosity led me farther on to rue Paul Bert, where I noticed a bistro at number 18 filled with delightful sounds that captured my attention. It was 12:45 p.m., the height of the lunch rush, and I felt an irresistible urge to step inside. The atmosphere was lively, filled with loud voices, chatter, and laughter, and it smelled deliciously good!

I was greeted by a cheerful family atmosphere. It was the kind of bistro where meals seemed to linger for an eternity, creating a precious suspension of time, and where a deep connection with friends inspires ideas. As I leaned on the counter, I ordered a glass of Muscadet from Jo Landron, and my attention was drawn to the menu of the day written in chalk on the slate:

- Starter: Warm spring leeks from Le Perche, Domaine Gramenon black truffle vinaigrette
- Main: Milk-fed calf's liver Grenoble-style, steamed potatoes in their skins
- Dessert: The famous Paris-Brest, made in house by chef Thierry

The menu had style, substance, and character! I had entered an authentic Parisian bistro! I then looked at the wine list that had been presented to me as if it were a gift: Dard et Ribo, Overnoy, Lapierre, Binner, Arena, champagne Jacques Lassaigne, Magnon, Souhaut, Meylet, Breton, Prieuré-Roch, Puzelat, Foillard, and so many others. It was a parade of all the pioneers of natural wines—a true work of art!

By this point, I was feeling hungry and thirsty, so I decided to sit next to a table of lively characters who appeared to be long-time regulars. As I looked down at their plates, I admired the impeccable presentation of their meals. Each dish arrived in perfect tempo, without the slightest fault in its appeal. I felt overjoyed at the prospect of my meal, and the bottle of Mémé 1999 from Domaine Gramenon that I was enjoying helped me feel more at ease to get to know this group of lunch companions. It was indeed a memorable experience, like a scene straight out of the cult classic *Les Tontons Flingueurs*, whose cast included Lino Ventura, Bernard Blier, Francis Blanche, and Jean Lefebvre. I felt as if I were seated next to the film's characters themselves, captivated by their playful humor and expressions. The delightful combination of wine and food heightened my emotions, making me feel as if I had been transported back to a time when friendship was first invented! The group included Michel, a former tool salesman turned restaurateur; Patrick, a film producer; Bernard, a wine merchant; and Bertrand, the bistro's owner. Within this short span of time, I listened to them redefine the world of hospitality, media, and politics with conviction and, above all, a deliberate impudence that made me writhe with laughter. Their dialogue captured the wit and irreverence of the film's great screenwriter Paul Audiard: opinionated but never rude, frank but true, and displaying an impertinent elegance. The discussions were often a little loud but never out of place. As Georges Brassens sings, "they were not sons of bitches, but friends as good as you could get, and friends first of all." As customers finished their meal and left, they greeted the table just as one greets family members. More than one person extended them a "See you tomorrow!" which said a lot about the life of this bistro. I could have been in the theater, or even in heaven, but I was at Bistrot Paul Bert, at Gwen and Bertrand's place, and it was damn grand!

After departing, I immediately called my papa, who lives in Pau, to share that, after long months of research, I had finally found Paris's beating heart!

GWEN
& BERTRAND

It is up to me, Bertrand, to capture the following thoughts in text. Gwen and I discussed the matter with Annabelle Schachmes and my editor. While the choice for me to do so seemed obvious to them, the task felt impossible to me. However, they were somewhat convincing, so I will start by trying to convey the essence of my other half, G. C. (Gwen Cadoret). Her first name, Gwénaëlle, reflects her Breton heritage, and her family name, Cadoret, reveals her DNA. Gwen comes from several generations of oyster farmers along the Belon River who were not only ocean farmers but mayors and deputies during the Third Republic. They were known for their tenacity and entrepreneurial spirit. Her great-grandfather, grandfather, father, and now her brother have all continued the tradition of promoting the exceptional oysters from this small corner of Brittany.

Gwen's strong character, work ethic, and desire to build an enduring family were directly influenced by her upbringing. Although I had always been friends with her brother and parents, a romantic relationship between us seemed unlikely due to our different ages and situations. However, life from time to time takes unexpected turns to reach its intended purpose. Even after the loss of a loved one, life can take over and present us with new opportunities. My and Gwen's meeting was one such opportunity. Let's make this a short story: What was once improbable became probable, what was once probable became certain, and what was once certain became a reality.

Thirty years, two wonderful kids, and three restaurants later, when I look around today, Gwen is still beside me. Without her, nothing would have been possible; nothing would have been the same. She is a tireless worker and, even more, a wonderful and admirable mother. Gwen has been the punctuation in our lives, knowing where to place the commas and what to put in parentheses as superfluous in order to create focus and meaning to our work, all while never forgetting her family. But let's not get too carried away. It wasn't perfect every day, but plates never went flying.

CONTENTS

P. 14

INTRODUCTION

P. 30

ENTRÉES (APPETIZERS)

P. 98

PLATS (MAINS)

P. 174

L'ÉCAILLER DU BISTROT

RECIPES FROM OUR SEAFOOD-FOCUSED RESTAURANT NEXT DOOR TO LE BISTROT PAUL BERT

P. 196

ACCOMPANIMENTS & SAUCES

P. 224

DESSERTS

A BISTRO
IS A JOURNEY TAKEN IN PLACE

A bistro should feel like a home away from home. And in many ways, it becomes a second home. The familiar sounds and aromas of food cooking intermingled with those of coffee freshly brewing take me back to my home as a child when the barstools seemed so high and I would carefully watch the dice of a game of 421 roll across the Dubonnet carpet. The baskets of bread and the decanters lined up on the bistro's shelves remind me of my toy soldiers I had as a boy. A typical day at the bistro begins with Nathalie checking the folds of the tablecloth, finding the perfect spot for the pepper mill, and smoothing out her apron. The chef leans against the passthrough from the kitchen with only his head visible. He is the captain of this ship, smiling at the first arrivals while grumbling "They're already here!" Thomas greets them with a nod. Those arriving include an improbable American French couple, a renowned architect who slips behind his regular table at number 14, an old carpenter and his dog from the neighborhood, and two twenty-something Japanese women who photograph each other as soon as they sit down. The chef ducks back into the kitchen, grumbling under his breath. The pots and pans clatter as he sharpens his knives against a background of running water. The buzz has started! Let service begin!

A Parisian bistro is all this: noises, smells, glances, and voices that overlap and respond to one another across tables.

We are in Paris, deep in its heart. The stage is set, making you feel you are where you belong. The white cloth napkins are neatly folded as they should be. An old friend of mine once said, "I love cloth napkins; it must be my feminine side. I appreciate the beautiful linen and the softness of the fabric. Let's leave the paper napkins to the greasy spoons and for more hygienic uses!"

The Thonet chairs and the black leatherette banquettes with their tired upholstery, shaped by generations of posteriors, catch your eye. The pewter bar reflects the relationships it has witnessed, as the immortal French writer Antoine Blondin, prince of Parisian bistros and lover of the almighty bottle, once said.

But let's get down to business. The chalk slate takes us on a journey through France: beef tongue from Normandy, oysters from Belon, lettuces from the bistro's garden. The choices reflect the countryside, and the dishes take us on a journey through the seasons. The *oeufs mayonnaise* are embellished with wild garlic. Is truffle season already over? The coquilles Saint Jacques have left, and we now look forward to leafy greens, olive oil, and sunshine. A strong aroma fills the air from the abundance of cheeses that blend on plates as customers awkwardly navigate them with their knives, mingling goat with cow. The sheep is well represented in the Roquefort, which sweats a little, while the aged Mimolette remains composed.

Corks are popping, and wine flows into glasses, enhancing the elegance of the tablecloth with their vibrant colors. The wines—most of which are natural, though not all—are offered in bottles, and occasionally as magnums. Depending on your mood, you might choose a white or red, light and fruity, from the Côte du Py to the Luberon; or opt for an orange and oxidative wine, depending on your day's companion; or maybe choose with a fickle finger or by familiarity. You might savor them while alone or with company, and maybe silently, respectfully, and intellectually. There will always be those who scrutinize the hundreds of labels that make up the wine list, hoping to find a deal and end up asking why we don't have Château something-or-other available.

As time passes, the volume rises, energy intensifies, legs brush against each other under the tables, and eyes begin to sparkle. Now it's time to collect yourself and move on to sweeter things. There are no dainty petits fours offered here, just classic desserts of true substance! Selections combine fruit and sugar, puff pastry and pastry cream, and farm-fresh cream and strawberries, among the many choices.

Next, it's time for *un café*! It's a magical moment when everything feels at stake. The foam on the cappuccino must stand high. A distinct aroma builds and permeates the room. The burning liquid distills into touches of dark chocolate and burnt wood with a bitter edge. We are now transported to Haiti or Brazil.

What a journey from the rue Paul Bert to Rio via the green landscape of Le Perche and the Breton estuaries. I got to dream and travel for the price of a meal. I'll be back, that's for sure. I already feel at home.

The bistro is a theater with two performances a day. Our work, our duty, our passion has only one raison d'être: to make people feel happier than when they arrived!

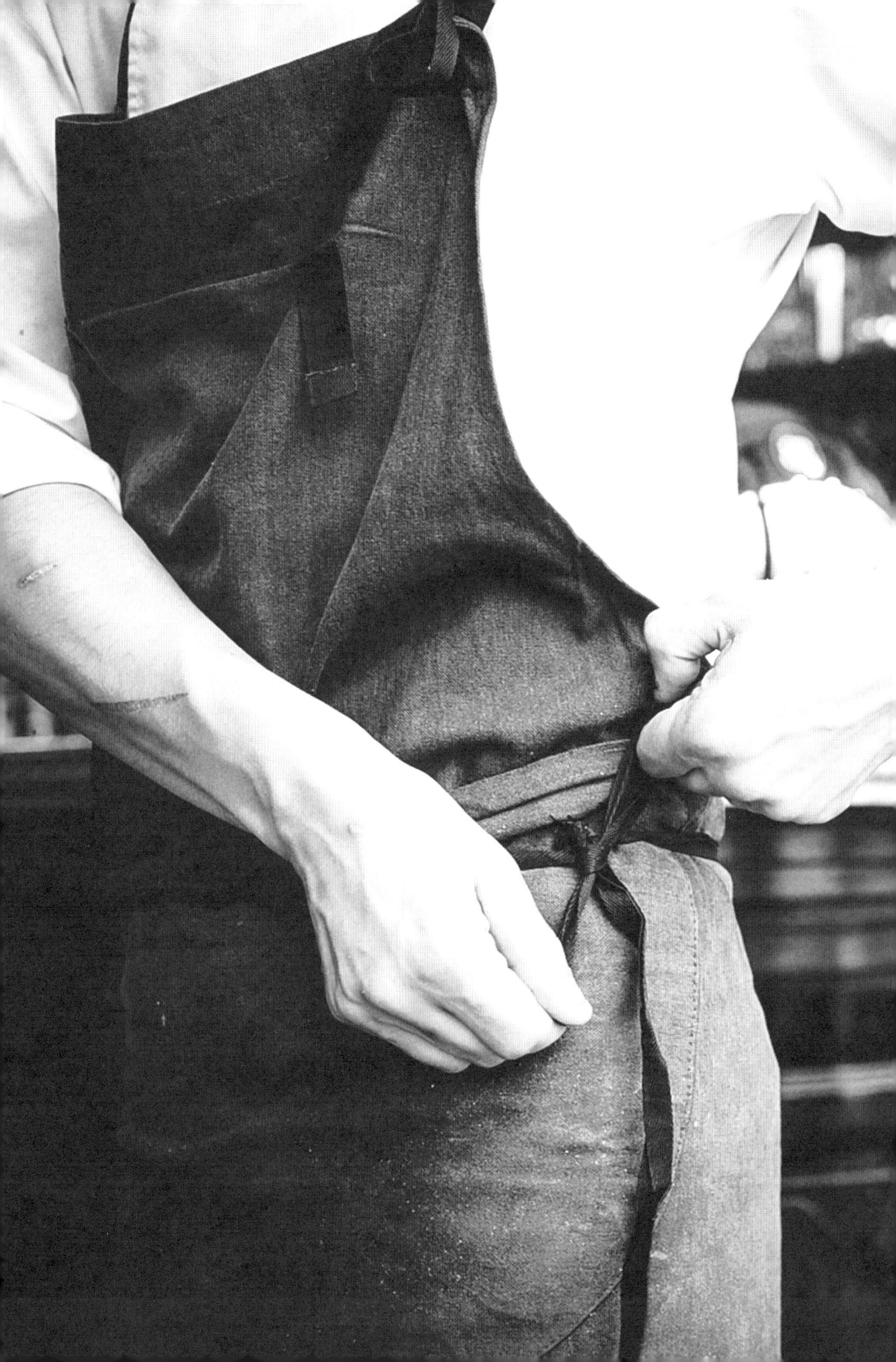

AND BISTROT PAUL BERT
CAME INTO OUR LIVES . . .

I looked through the window of a closed bistro at 18 rue Paul Bert. A weary-looking man was sitting alone behind the bar, the door shut, pretending not to notice me. The cleaning lady stepped out with a bag of garbage and shouted to me, “It’s closed. It’s going to be up for sale soon. If you’re interested, I can give you the owner’s number. He has a brasserie in Saint-Germain-en-Laye.”

Without really believing what she said, I dialed the number. At the other end of the line, a gravelly voice asked, “What’s this about?” The conversation was short and to the point. “If you’re that interested, just come and see me. I’ll see you in an hour.” As the RER train pulled out of the Paris station, Gwénaëlle and I were in a cheerful mood despite this mode of travel not being our cup of tea. We had no idea this short train trip out of Paris, from Place de la Nation to Saint-Germain-en-Laye, would change our lives. It doesn’t take much to tempt fate: an abandoned-looking bistro, a well-meaning caretaker, a quick phone call, and an impromptu appointment, and there we were, standing in front of a café-tabac-maison-de-la-presse (a type of coffee shop/gift shop/card shop). The owner, whose voice I recognized from over the phone, was behind the bar, prominently situated to the right of the cash register. As soon as we pushed open the door, he greeted us with, “So Parisians, the train isn’t that bad! So, you’re interested in my café on rue Paul Bert?” His boisterous voice was tinged with a strong Aveyron accent, and his hands were as large as eggbeaters. His eyes scrutinized us with both astonishment and gentleness. It was clear we had to be straightforward with him. He pointed out that we were not “from the country.” “It’s a shame, really.” But after a short interrogation, he concluded we were “Bretons,” and it was “better than nothing and no worse than anything else.”

He recounted the story of his café and when he left the Aveyron to move north to the capital and of his place on rue Paul Bert, where he became a café owner and *charbonnier* (coal peddler). The Auvergnats operated these “wine and coal cafés,” while also sometimes becoming scrap merchants, when they migrated to Paris due to lack of work at home. At the time, the Auvergnats bourgeoisie were farmers. Others lived in poverty and had no choice but to leave home to find work. His wife ran the tiny café where she sold many glasses of Avèze (an herby Aveyron liqueur). She had become, according to rumors, the best seller of this beverage in the region. During this time, her husband was one of the coal peddlers. Trains would arrive at night at the Gare de Lyon, where coal was purchased by the carload.

The coal had to be quickly transferred to trucks before the train departed at its appointed time. If the train car was not emptied in time, well, that was too bad for the *charbonnier*! Once back at rue Paul Bert, the trucks were unloaded at the rear, and the coal was then bagged for delivery throughout Paris. The sacks were always carried on men's backs and through the back service stairs of businesses. The days were long, and the work was exhausting, but despite being covered in dust and worn out at the end of the day, they were considered the new Aveyron aristocracy. Through their hard work, courage, respect for traditions, and cultivation of their roots, the Auvergnats successfully established themselves in the capital as operators of cafés and brasseries within a carefully regulated environment. Their marriages, if not arranged, were at least suggested. Their names—the Combettes, the Costes brothers, the Allo family, and many others—resonate on Paris's streets as successful entrepreneurial families.

He shared all of this with me over the following weeks during the purchase of what was to become Bistrot Paul Bert. This was at the end of 1996. And not only did he hand over the business to us in excellent condition, but more importantly, in my eyes, he gave me his friendship and trust. Throughout the process, he would pick me up on Wednesdays to take me to lunch at an Aveyron café in Bercy. There, he would meet friends who owned bistros, whether they were wealthy or poor, all of whom were bons vivants enjoying plates of *aligot* (mashed potatoes with cheese) as red wine flowed freely. He introduced me in a casual manner: "He's Breton," adding, "it's better than nothing," and after a pause, he continued, "I sold him my bistro. He just has to work hard." At that moment, the die had been cast. I felt as though I had been knighted, with a wineglass in my right hand, a slice of sausage in my left, and two friendly slaps on the back, followed by a cheerful, "Go get 'em." In what felt like a novel, I was living the simple yet grand stories of this provincial microcosm that held the reins of my profession.

During this time, opinions and advice flew at me from all directions: "This regulation isn't right! Don't forget to talk to Jacques about it!" "Above all, if you go to Ussel, be sure to talk to Jacques!" I soon realized they were referring to then President Jacques Chirac. Whether in ties or checkered shirts, suspenders or clogs, these were individuals of power and political savvy, all managing their responsibilities smoothly from behind their counters. Despite the countless hours of work, they always prioritized respect and friendship, a practice we now refer to as "lobbying." This environment was beginning to appeal to me.

8 DAYS
BEFORE OPENING . . .

We were opening in eight days. Everything was ready! The kitchen was fixed up using the old stove found on site. New pots and pans gleamed along the kitchen's stainless-steel shelves. My friend Jean-Louis Bravo, from the Brocante d'Epinay, a salvage mecca for everything imaginable that can transform a bistro of today into an old-fashioned one, delivered a truck of Thonet chairs, tables, bar shelves, brass columns, and old posters.

In just a few hours, we would be armed with sponges, cleaning soaps, brushes, and an array of paint cans and varnish bottles, ready to follow the orders of our friend and decorator Pierre Sabria, a specialist in making the new appear old again. The coat of paint aged instantly, giving the impression that it had been there forever, as if it were tinted by years of cigarette smoke and kitchen aromas. The embossed floral wallpaper, which I found horrendous, vanished beneath layers of paint and the varnish crackled under the warm air of a skillfully wielded hair dryer. Each hour of work took Paul Bert back in time under the steady gaze of a decorator who executed impeccable coats of paint and perfect finishes. Everything was in place. The banquettes reupholstered in the old style had been delivered. The antique chandeliers were hooked up to current standards. Everything seemed perfect. Well, not quite, just one detail, or maybe two, were not exactly right within this tableau: First, the bank accounts were empty, and second, I totally forgot to order the dishes and glassware. I attempted to get two urgent quotes from a supplier. The answer was a punch to the gut! "We don't know you, so we need payment on delivery!" We were eight days away from the opening! It was Friday at 6 p.m. I tried to get my brain working, which clearly refused to get going. They say ideas come to you as you sleep, but that was not the case this time. I had to urgently come up with 50,000 francs. I reflected on the situation in front of a lukewarm cup of coffee as bitter as my circumstances.

Suddenly, Gwénaëlle shook me out of my daze and reminded me that we were invited to lunch at a friend's house who is an antique dealer in Béthune and that it was high time we made a visit. I agreed, as nothing could be accomplished that day anyway. While driving, I made the decision to tell her about my concerns. We are very close, so I had nothing to lose.

Lunch with our friends was joyful and delicious, extending through dessert. Just as I was about to share my problem, my friend began recounting his story about a problem that was putting him in a tough financial position. I felt deflated inside, and I didn't want to add anything more to complicate his situation. The bottle of champagne his wife opened for dessert tasted as bitter as my morning coffee. However, there are days when the planets align despite everything, and days when the gods play with us just to remind us they exist.

Véronique, his wife, while filling my coupe for the second time, said to me, "Philippe told me that you were opening soon. Your work must be done. Of course, you can count on us to be there for the opening." Nervously, and without thinking, I replied, "I just have the dishes and glasses left to buy and it's good." My friend turned to me and said, "Don't buy anything. My grandfather sold factory seconds of dishes and glasses, and there are still plenty of them available at a discount." We spent the weekend opening boxes that had been sealed since the 1940s and discovered plates of all sizes plus wine, water, and liqueur glasses. We left with a loaded car and a light heart. Philippe arrived with a second delivery the following Wednesday. I still didn't really believe in God, but in Bacchus, definitely.

SALLE
au
FOND

PAUL BERT

FROM MICHEL PICARD
TO BISTRONOMY

Michel Picard was more than just a man to me. He was history, a legend.

Michel entered my life like a meteorite one day in February 1998. It was 1:55 p.m. when three sketchy characters showed up for lunch. Among them, one person immediately stood out. He wore a blue-checked shirt unbuttoned over a white T-shirt with jeans held up by suspenders. He had a baby face, was a little chubby, and sported a sarcastic smile. "It seems that you serve food," he remarked as he settled in. Once seated, he anxiously examined a paper napkin, which he had fastened with two clips to a chain around his neck. I will never forget that look from him, where his compassion for me was matched only by a palpable irritation, clearly indicating his disdain for that paper napkin.

A customer discreetly called out to me at the bar, saying, "Watch out! It's Michel Picard, the pain in the neck from restaurant Astier." My heart raced; I hadn't recognized him. Years ago, he kicked me out of his restaurant for being ten minutes past service time when I had raced across Paris during a time when mobile phones were still a distant idea in our imaginations, and automobiles, having just replaced horse-drawn buggies, caused traffic jams nearly as unbearable as the ones we experience today thanks to the mayor of Paris's impressive governance.

After he was seated, I planted myself firmly in front of his table, noticing that my watch read 2:25 p.m. (At that time, we served lunch until 2:30 p.m. Today it's until 2:00 p.m.—everything is going downhill.) Without any hint of irony and with a total lack of goodwill—something my detractors would say is typical of me—I said, "Sorry, gentlemen, it's 2:30 p.m. Lunch service is over."

He glanced down at his watch and replied, "Ha! Ha! Ha! You must have been kicked out of my place! All is fair."

Needless to say, we served them anyway. As expected, he complained about everything. He returned once, ten times, a hundred times—almost every day, sometimes even twice in one day! He began to feel at home, and we became friends.

Michel Picard embarked on his professional career in the 1980s, far from the restaurant industry. At that time, he worked in a tool shop dedicated to artisans on Avenue de la République. Passionate about good food, he set up a kitchen on the first floor, a sort of table d'hôte, where he regularly prepared meals for his staff and salesmen, who quickly became accustomed to his cooking. At that time, he referred to himself as a dealer in bolts and wrenches. His small business enjoyed an extremely respectable success.

Beneath his suave appearance lay an innate business instinct. His establishment quickly became a must-visit for his clientele of craftsmen and small-business entrepreneurs thanks to the quality of the post-sales service he offered. Although I didn't know him then, I sense he was bored. He was a regular at a local pub where Madame Astier, whose name was proudly displayed on the sign, was in charge. One day, as she lamented about the annoying customers, her back pain, the passage of time, and the hours spent in front of her stovetop, Michel, without thinking and between sips of whisky—a beverage he was particularly fond of—responded, "Stop complaining, Madame Astier. I will buy your bistro from you on the condition that you stay on."

Months passed, and it became time to move on from his tool shop and pass it on to his employees. He then found himself in the kitchen and in charge of "Chez Astier." At first, Madame Astier was by his side, but soon after he was alone in the kitchen. This new business venture was a genius move for him. He transformed the bistro, located deep within Paris's 11th arrondissement, into a place that became known to all Parisians, if not the entire world.

In 1981, Michel popularized the *menu-carte*, which could be easily rolled out. This concept included a choice of a starter, main dish, cheese platter, and dessert, all for a fixed price, challenging his competitors' traditional offerings. The paternity for this innovative restaurant practice is shared between bistro Astier and Yves Camdeborde at his iconic bistro, La Régalade, in the 14th arrondissement. I will refrain from choosing between them; they were good friends with each other and had become mine.

Yves, a talented chef who trained under Christian Constant—at the time a three-star Michelin chef leading the kitchens at the Hôtel de Crillon—was also instrumental in the development of what my friend Sébastien Demorand would later coin "bistronomy," defined as bringing high-quality cuisine to neighborhood bistros in a friendly atmosphere at affordable prices. This idea involves using the same ingredients and techniques found in Michelin-starred restaurants, executed by young chefs from haute cuisine. The goal is to create a dining experience free from the heaviness and constraints of formal etiquette, which had long been dictated by the "General Commander," the *Guide Michelin*.

Bistronomy quickly gained recognition through articles written by François Simon, a prominent journalist for *Le Figaro*, who praised this new generation of chef-restaurateurs. Appreciation for this new dining approach reached its peak with his impactful column titled "Those Forgotten by Michelin," published the week after the Michelin guide was released.

This new vision of gastronomy, more in tune with today's society, was embraced by Yves Camdeborde, Thierry Faucher, Thierry Breton, Éric Fréchon, and several others, including Rodolphe Paquin. Rodolphe was one of Michel's closest associates and played a significant role in this culinary evolution. They would all often gather late at night after their shifts to dine together at Astier, then move on to Le Villaret, the last restaurant founded by Michel that has since become a cult favorite. Today, it is masterfully run by Olivier Gaslain, Michel's clever son, alongside his wife. Michel Picard taught me everything about the restaurant business, service, wines, and the concept of bistronomy before it even had that name. He became my mentor, and I was his devoted shadow. Through these encounters and the values of generosity, sharing, kindness, hard work, and respect they embodied, Bistrot Paul Bert became what it is today. I could continue to elaborate on these topics with anecdotes and compliments, but to avoid boring you, I'll conclude by recounting a story about this incredible man and everyone around him.

We had weekly meetings on Mondays for lunch and there might be three, five, or ten of us, but we never skipped the chance to meet. Starting on Friday, Michel would call the group, choose a location, book a table, and take note of anyone who couldn't attend—worse, still, of those who forgot to cancel. Our meetings might even take place at the local *tabac* or at Pierre Gagnaire's restaurant where Gagnaire referred to Michel as "the inspector." Like a scene from a Claude Sautet film, we would arrive as if stepping onto a stage, but not without first responding in the affirmative to the critical question, "You didn't forget to stop by the ATM?" It was out of the question to not pay a fellow restaurateur in cash.

Bernard the wine merchant, with his horizontal mustache, was present. So was Patrick, the former executive film producer and restaurateur, who could list, without batting an eyelash, the forty-three dishes he had recently eaten at the famous so-and-so's, but which, in truth, only had five items on its menu. Then there was the famous Barrio, a music producer and enlightened lover of pretty women. The blonde Delphine, who was like a daughter to him, often came along with her cousin, whom we all loved. Among the group were the chefs, many from the new bistronomy generation: Yves Camdeborde, Thierry Breton, Thierry Faucher, and Rodolphe Paquin, nick-named "the fourth musketeer" and the only one who didn't come from the Crillon. Also present were winemakers, butchers, and other bons vivants. They were all honest drinkers and, according to some, avid gossipers! Finally, there were the primary beneficiaries of this event—Gwénaëlle, my better half, and myself—intimidated by this rowdy group of hungry, thirsty individuals. They were always ready to criticize but equally capable of unlim-ited praise, depending on their moods and the number of empty bottles at the table. We quickly got up to speed.

These lunches served as a condensed introduction to a profession I knew little about. They also allowed me to meet remarkable individuals who were full of humanity and generosity, and for whom the words work, rigor, prod-ucts, and seasons were synonymous with pleasure, conviviality, and respect, among other things. Without these lunches, without Michel, and without all of them—including those who are sadly no longer with us—Gwen and I would not have become the restaurateurs we are today, and the reputation of Bistrot Paul Bert would never have extended beyond the corner of the street.

Shop the
collection online
on giftshop.club
CHAMPAGNE
aurent Perrier
REIMS
KRUG
CHAMPAGNE

HENRIOT
REIMS
NAMUR-PERRIER

(APPETIZERS)

RÉES

OEUFS MAYONNAISE

(*Boiled Eggs with Mayonnaise*)

Serves 2

Preparation time: 5 minutes
Cooking time: 7 minutes

---

4 medium organic eggs
Scant ½ cup (100 g) Mayonnaise *(page 211)*

1 • Bring a large saucepan of water to a boil. Add the eggs and cook for 7 minutes. Transfer the eggs to a strainer and place them under cold running water to immediately stop the cooking.

2 • Peel the eggs and cut them in half. Place 4 halves on each of 2 serving plates. Pipe or spoon the mayonnaise onto each half.

Tip: Choose toppings according to the season. For example, serve with a little shaved truffle, some thinly sliced wild garlic or chives, a few pieces of fish roe, or taramasalata topped with a few salmon eggs. In the restaurant, we often rest the eggs on a little Céleri Rémoulade (page 65) to keep them from moving on the plate and serve them with a small green salad.

PAUL BERT
BISTROT
PAUL BERT

LE BISTROT
PAUL BERT
LE BISTROT
PAUL BERT

OEUFS AU PLAT

(*Eggs Sunny-Side Up*)

Serves 2

Preparation time: 5 minutes (if making a side accompaniment)
Cooking time: 11 to 13 minutes

3½ tablespoons (50 g) unsalted butter
4 medium organic eggs
Salt and pepper to taste

1 • Heat 1½ tablespoons of the butter in a medium skillet over low heat. Do not let the butter brown to ensure the eggs cook gently and evenly. Cook 2 eggs at a time: Add 2 eggs to the pan at once and increase the heat slightly. Cook for 5 to 6 minutes, just until the whites are uniformly cooked and the yolks are warmed through but not firm.

2 • Transfer the cooked eggs to a serving plate, then add the remaining 2 tablespoons butter to the pan and repeat the steps with the remaining eggs.

Tip: Choose accompaniments according to the season, such as shaved black truffle, panfried morels or porcini mushrooms, or thin slices of Prince de Paris *jambon blanc* or another superior-quality cooked ham.

HARENGS POMME À L'HUILE

NOUVELLE GÉNÉRATION

(New-Style Pickled Herring with Potatoes)

Serves 2

Preparation time: 15 minutes
Cooking time: 15 minutes
Resting time: 5 minutes

---

6 yellow fingerling potatoes (we use Ratte potatoes, but you can substitute for your preferred local variety)
1 sprig dill
½ red onion
2 heaping tablespoons crème fraîche
2 smoked pickled herring fillets
2 teaspoons trout roe
Salt and freshly ground black pepper
Neutral-flavor oil

1 • Rinse the potatoes under cold running water. Brush them, if needed, to remove any excess dirt. Rinse the dill under a slow stream of cold water, then thoroughly pat it dry using paper towels. Peel the onion and thinly slice it into rings.

2 • Bring a medium saucepan of water to a boil. Add the potatoes and cook over medium heat for about 15 minutes, until tender when pierced with a fork. Drain and let cool at room temperature for 5 minutes, then slice the potatoes into rounds about ⅕ inch (5 mm) thick.

3 • Transfer the potato rounds to a bowl and add the crème fraîche. Season with salt and pepper. Carefully stir the potatoes to evenly coat them.

4 • Arrange a row of potatoes and crème fraîche on each of 2 serving plates. Place a herring fillet on top of each row of potatoes and drizzle a little oil on top. Neatly arrange some chopped dill, trout roe, and rings of onion on top of each fillet and serve.

PAUL BERT

OEUFS EN MEURETTE

(Poached Eggs in Red Wine Sauce)

Serves 2

Preparation time: 10 minutes
Cooking time: 30 minutes

---

1 shallot
1 bunch grelot onions (or use 10 to 12 pearl onions)
5¼ ounces (150 g) white button mushrooms
7 ounces (200 g) lardons
1½ tablespoons unsalted butter
1 cup (250 ml) red wine
1 bouquet garni (see Tip)
Freshly ground black pepper
2 large eggs
⅔ cup (150 ml) distilled white vinegar

1 • Peel the shallot and onions. Finely chop the shallot. Briefly rinse the mushrooms under cold running water and cut off the rough ends from their stems. Quarter the mushrooms.

2 • In a large skillet over high heat, fry the lardons for 2 or 3 minutes, until crisp. Add the butter, onions, and shallot to the pan. Stir with a wooden spoon and cook for 2 to 3 minutes, until the onions and shallot are softened. Deglaze the pan with the wine, then add the bouquet garni. Season with pepper. Add the mushrooms and cook uncovered for about 20 minutes to reduce. Remove the bouquet garni and set the pan aside off the heat.

3 • Break each egg into its own small ramekin. Bring a saucepan of water to a boil. Add the vinegar to the water. As soon as the water is boiling, stir it with a wooden spoon in a clockwise direction to create a gentle swirl. When the water is swirling, hold the ramekins just above the surface of the water and gently pour in the eggs. Cook for 4 minutes, or until the whites are set and the yolks are at your desired doneness. Remove the eggs using a slotted spoon and transfer to a paper towel–lined plate to drain completely.

4 • Spoon a little of the mushroom mixture into each of 2 shallow serving bowls. Place a poached egg on top of each and serve.

Tip: Make a bouquet garni by creating a bundle of different herbs, such as parsley, thyme, and bay leaves, tied with kitchen twine. Remove before serving.

ASPERGES VERTES RÔTIES

AU LARD CROUSTILLANT

(Roasted Green Asparagus with Crispy Bacon)

Serves 2

Preparation time: 5 minutes
Cooking time: 20 minutes
Resting time: 30 minutes

4 slices bacon
6 medium (not too thin) spears green asparagus
3½ tablespoons (50 g) unsalted butter
⅔ cup (150 ml) chicken stock
Salt and freshly ground black pepper
1 cup (250 ml) Vinaigrette *(page 210)*

1 • Preheat the oven to 350°F (180°C).

2 • Arrange the bacon slices on a baking sheet lined with parchment paper. Cover the slices with a piece of parchment paper, then place a baking sheet on top to help keep the slices from curling up while baking. Bake for 10 minutes, until crisp. Let cool for 30 minutes at room temperature.

3 • Cut off ⅓ to 1 inch (1 to 3 cm) of the rough end of each asparagus spear. Rinse the asparagus under cold running water. Thoroughly pat them dry using paper towels.

4 • Melt the butter in a large skillet over medium heat. Add the stock and asparagus. Decrease the heat to low and cook for 10 minutes, turning them frequently to ensure they are evenly browned on all sides. Set aside off the heat.

5 • Arrange 3 asparagus spears on each of 2 serving plates and season with salt and pepper. Place 2 pieces of the crisp bacon on top. Serve with the vinaigrette.

LE BISTROT
PAUL BERT

SALADE DE HARICOTS VERTS

CROÛTONS, COPEAUX DE PARMESAN ET PIGNONS TORRÉFIÉS

(Green Bean Salad, Croutons, Parmesan Shavings, Toasted Pine Nuts)

Serves 2

Preparation time: 10 minutes
Cooking time: 10 minutes
Resting time: 10 minutes

---

2 chives

1 slice white sandwich bread, slightly stale, crust removed

Olive oil

⅓ cup (50 g) pine nuts

10½ ounces (300 g) haricots verts

1¾ ounces (50 g) Parmesan cheese

Apple cider vinegar

Fleur de sel sea salt

Freshly ground black pepper

1 • Rinse the chives under a slow stream of cold water. Thoroughly pat them dry using a paper towel, then finely chop them. Cut the bread into small cubes. Heat a drizzle of oil in a medium skillet over high heat. Add the bread cubes and pine nuts and cook for 3 to 4 minutes, just until lightly toasted. Set aside on a paper towel–lined plate.

2 • Bring a saucepan of water to a boil. Add the haricots verts and cook over medium heat for 6 minutes, until bright green and tender. Immediately transfer the beans to a bowl of ice water to stop the cooking. Let rest for 10 minutes, then thoroughly drain them.

3 • Using a vegetable peeler, shave the Parmesan into thin shavings.

4 • Neatly arrange the beans on 2 serving plates. Generously drizzle the beans with oil, then add a drizzle of vinegar. Sprinkle on the chives, pine nuts, and croutons. Top with several Parmesan shavings. Season with sea salt and pepper.

SALADE DE HARICOTS BEURRE

CROÛTONS ET COPEAUX DE FOIE GRAS

(Yellow Bean Salad, Croutons, Foie Gras Shavings, Toasted Pine Nuts)

Serves 2

Preparation time: 10 minutes
Cooking time: 10 minutes
Resting time: 10 minutes

½ bunch chives
1 slice white sandwich bread, slightly stale, crust removed
Olive oil
⅓ cup (50 g) pine nuts
10½ ounces (300 g) yellow beans
1¾ ounces (50 g) goose or duck foie gras
Red or white wine vinegar
Fleur de sel sea salt
Freshly ground black pepper

1 • Rinse the chives under a slow stream of cold water. Thoroughly pat them dry using a paper towel, then finely chop them. Cut the bread into small cubes. Heat a drizzle of oil in a medium skillet over high heat. Add the bread cubes and pine nuts and cook for 3 to 4 minutes, just until lightly toasted. Set aside on a paper towel–lined plate.

2 • Bring a saucepan of water to a boil. Add the beans and cook over medium heat for 6 minutes. Immediately transfer the beans to a bowl of ice water to stop the cooking. Let rest for 10 minutes, then thoroughly drain them.

3 • Using a vegetable peeler, shave the foie gras into thin shavings. Refrigerate until needed.

4 • Neatly arrange the beans on 2 serving plates. Generously drizzle the beans with oil, then add a drizzle of vinegar. Sprinkle on the chives, pine nuts, and croutons. Top with several foie gras shavings. Season with sea salt and pepper.

LE BISTROT
PAUL BERT

PAUL BERT

SALADE DE TOMATES DU JARDIN

(*Garden Tomato Salad*)

Serves 2

Preparation time: 15 minutes

---

2 chives
4 heirloom tomatoes of different sizes and colors (we often use grappe, green zebra, or pineapple, but find your own local varieties)
1 red onion
1 peach
2 sprigs basil
Olive oil
Fleur de sel sea salt
Freshly ground black pepper

1 • Rinse the chives and tomatoes under cold running water. Thoroughly pat them dry. Finely chop the chives. Remove the stems and cores from the tomatoes and slice the tomatoes. Peel the onion and peach and thinly slice them.

2 • On 2 serving plates, arrange the slices of tomatoes and peach and the torn basil leaves into stacks, alternating the ingredients and making sure to top each with some basil. Use a stainless-steel cooking ring, if desired, to assist with neatly stacking the slices. Drizzle generously with oil. Add the sliced onion on top and sprinkle with the chives. Season with sea salt and pepper.

ARTICHAUTS VINAIGRETTE

(*Artichokes with Vinaigrette*)

Serves 2

Preparation time: 5 minutes
Cooking time: About 1 hour

Salt

1 organic lemon

2 globe artichokes (we often use Camus de Bretagne but any large artichoke will do)

2 chives

½ shallot

Just over ¾ cup (200 ml) Vinaigrette *(page 210)*

1 • Bring a large pot of salted water to a boil. Snap off the tough outer leaves of the artichoke. Using a serrated knife, cut off the top third of each artichoke. Peel the stems to remove the tough outer layer and trim the stems so that the artichokes can sit upright. Halve the lemon and squeeze the juice into the boiling water. You can also place the lemon peel into the pot. Add the artichokes. Cook over low heat, covered, for about 40 minutes to 1 hour (which can vary according to the size of the artichokes), until the stem is tender when pierced with a fork and the leaves feel loose and easy to remove. Set the artichokes aside top side down for several minutes to drain.

2 • Rinse the chives under a slow stream of cold water. Thoroughly pat them dry using a paper towel, then finely chop them. Peel and finely chop the shallot. Add the vinaigrette to 2 small serving dishes and sprinkle the chopped chives and shallot on top.

3 • Place an artichoke on each of the 2 serving plates and place the serving bowl of vinaigrette next to them for dipping. Serve.

Bistrot
Paul Bert
PAUL BERT

GOUGÈRES

(*Cheese Puffs*)

akes about 24 choux puffs

reparation time: 10 minutes
oking time: 35 minutes
esting time: 30 minutes

---

cup (250 ml) water
cup (250 ml) whole milk
cup plus 2 tablespoons (1¾ sticks/200 g) unsalted butter, cut into chunks
teaspoon salt
¼ cups plus 3 tablespoons (300 g) all-purpose flour
¾ ounces (50 g) Gruyère cheese, grated
large (350 g) eggs

1 • In a large saucepan, combine the water, milk, butter, and salt and bring to a boil. Add the flour a little at a time while whisking. Switch over to a wooden spoon and stir until a smooth dough forms. Continue to stir over low heat until the dough dries out a little and pulls away from the side of the pan, about 2 minutes. Immediately transfer the dough to the bowl of stand mixer fitted with the paddle attachment. Let cool for 1 minute. Begin beating on medium speed, then add the grated Gruyère. With the mixer running, add the eggs one at a time, beating well between each addition, until the mixture is smooth (it may separate but will come back together).

2 • Refrigerate for 30 minutes.

3 • Preheat the oven to 400°F (200°C).

4 • Line 2 baking sheets with silicone baking mats or parchment paper. Using a pastry bag fitted with a 1½-inch (4 cm) round pastry tube, pipe 12 uniform mounds on top of each.

5 • Bake for about 25 minutes, rotating the pans top to bottom and left to right halfway through, until crisp and golden.

FEUILLETÉ AU RIS DE VEAU

ASPERGES ET PETITS POIS

(Sweetbreads in Pastry, Asparagus, and Peas)

Serves 2

Preparation time: 10 minutes
Cooking time: 10 minutes

---

7 ounces (200 g) whole sweetbreads
2 shallots
1¾ ounces (50 g) white button mushrooms
4 or 5 medium spears green asparagus
1¾ ounces (50 g) sweet garden peas, preferably in the shell
1½ tablespoons unsalted butter
Neutral-flavor oil
3 tablespoons vin jaune or Savagnin wine
Scant ½ cup (100 ml) heavy cream
2 store-bought baked all-butter puff pastry shells

1 • Ask your butcher to remove the thin membran from around the sweetbreads or remove them usin a knife. Cut the sweetbreads into pieces. Peel and finely chop the shallots. Briefly rinse the mushroom under cold running water and cut off the rough end from their stems. Quarter the mushrooms. Cut off ⅓ to 1 inch (1 to 3 cm) of the rough end of each asparagus spear. Rinse the asparagus under cold running water. Shell the peas.

2 • Bring a medium pot of water to a boil. Boil the peas and asparagus just until cooked and they maintain slight firmness (see page 198). Immediately transfer them to a bowl of ice water to stop the cooking. Drain and then cut the asparagus into sections.

3 • In a large skillet over high heat, melt the butte with a drizzle of oil. Add the sweetbreads and cook just until light golden brown. Add the shallots and mushrooms. Deglaze the pan with the wine, then add the cream. Cook for 5 minutes while stirring continuously, until the sauce has thickened and the shallots and mushrooms are soft.

4 • Spoon the cooked sweetbreads into the puff pastry shells, then add the peas and asparagus. Serve.

SALADE DE LANGUE DE VEAU

ET POMMES DE TERRE

(Veal Tongue Salad with Potatoes)

Serves 2

Preparation time: 5 minutes
Cooking time: 3 hours 15 minutes
Resting time: 1 hour

- **carrot**
- **yellow onion**
- **sprig thyme**
- **bay leaf**
- **Salt**
- **small calf's tongue (about 1 pound 2 ounces/500 g)**
- **ounces (250 g) Ratte potatoes (or use yellow fingerling potatoes)**
- **½ red onion**
- **Freshly ground black pepper**
- **⅔ cup (150 ml) Vinaigrette** *(page 210)*

1 • Peel the carrot and onion. Place the carrot, onion, thyme, and bay leaf in a large pot with salted water. Bring to a boil over high heat.

2 • Add the tongue, ensuring it is fully submerged. Cook for 2 hours and 45 minutes, mostly covered, adding water occasionally if needed, until the tongue is tender and the skin will easily peel off. Set the cooked tongue aside to drain, then peel off the thin skin. Let cool for 1 hour at room temperature. Cut into small cubes and set aside.

3 • Bring a medium saucepan of water to a boil and add the potatoes. Cook over medium heat for 15 minutes, until soft when pierced with a fork. Drain the potatoes then peel them. Cut them into medium cubes.

4 • Peel and finely chop the onion. Place the tongue and potatoes in a bowl and season with salt and pepper. Add the vinaigrette and carefully stir to evenly coat the pieces.

5 • Neatly arrange the mixture on 2 serving plates. Add a few onion slices on top and serve.

CARPACCIO DE DAURADE

CITRON VERT ET FRUIT DE LA PASSION

(Sea Bream Carpaccio, Lime, and Passion Fruit)

Serves 2

Preparation time: 10 minutes

½ bunch chives
1 passion fruit
10½ ounces (300 g) sushi-grade sea bream fillet
Olive oil
Fleur de sel sea salt
½ organic lime

1 • Rinse the chives under a slow stream of cold water. Thoroughly dry them using a paper towel, then finely chop them. Halve the passion fruit and scoop out the seeds. Set the seeds aside.

2 • Very thinly slice the fillet and arrange the pieces neatly on 2 serving plates. Drizzle generously with oil. Sprinkle with the chives, passion fruit seeds, and a little sea salt. Grate some lime zest over the top.

Tip: You can replace the lime and passion fruit with grated cauliflower. If you choose this variation, use different colors of cauliflower for a colorful presentation.

LE BISTROT
PAUL BERT

LE BISTROT
PAUL BERT

FOIE GRAS

Serves 2

Preparation time: 10 minutes
Cooking time: 20 minutes
Resting time: 37½ hours

---

1 teaspoon salt, plus more for serving
1 teaspoon freshly ground black pepper, plus more for serving
Pinch freshly grated nutmeg
1 deveined goose or duck foie gras (about 14 ounces/400 g)
3 tablespoons Armagnac
Grilled bread, for serving
Chutney or jam, for serving

1 • In a small bowl, combine the salt, pepper, and nutmeg.

2 • Place a large piece of plastic wrap over a plate. The plastic wrap should extend about 2 inches (5 cm) beyond the edges of the plate. Place the foie gras on top, gently separating the 2 lobes of the foie gras, and season the lobes with the seasoning mixture on both sides. Drizzle the Armagnac over the tops of both lobes. Push the lobes back together, then wrap the foie gras tightly in the plastic wrap, twisting the ends so that it resembles a sausage. Place the wrapped foie gras on a second piece of plastic wrap and wrap it up in the same way. This will ensure the foie gras is sealed airtight. Set aside for 1 hour.

3 • Fill a large saucepan with water and set it over low heat. Using an instant-read thermometer, heat the water to 150°F (65°C). Place the wrapped foie gras in the hot water and cook for 20 minutes. Remove the foie gras and set it aside on a plate, still wrapped, to cool for 30 minutes at room temperature. Refrigerate for 36 hours.

4 • Slice the foie gras, season with salt and pepper, and serve with grilled bread and a jam or chutney of your choice.

CARPACCIO DE TÊTE DE VEAU

(*Veal Head Carpaccio*)

Serves 2

Preparation time: 10 minutes
Cooking time: 3 hours
Resting time: 24 hours

---

1 yellow onion
1 carrot
1 stalk celery
1 bouquet garni (see Tip, page 38)
Salt and freshly ground black pepper
1 small calf's head, trimmed by your butcher (approximately 3 pounds 5 ounces/1.5 kg)
1 small calf's tongue (about 1 pound 2 ounces/500 g)
4 sprigs tarragon

For the Sauce

½ shallot
3 anchovy fillets
1 teaspoon capers
3 chives

For the Toppings

Handful of arugula, chanterelles, and/or julienned radish (optional)

1 • Peel the onion and carrot. Rinse the celery stalk under cold running water.

2 • Bring a large pot of water to a boil. Add the onion, carrot, celery, and bouquet garni. Season with salt. Add the calf's head and tongue, ensuring they are fully submerged, adding more water if needed. Cook over low heat, covered, for 3 hours, until tender and the skin can easily peel off the tongue.

3 • Using a large skimmer or slotted spoon, remove the head and place it flat on a work surface. Remove any bones and large pieces of fat. Peel off the skin of the tongue. Season with salt and pepper.

4 • Rinse 2 tarragon sprigs under a slow stream of cold water. Thoroughly pat them dry. Spread the head out completely and place the tongue in the center along with the rinsed tarragon sprigs.

5 • Roll the head up around the tongue and tarragon. Wrap the head tightly in plastic wrap and refrigerate it for 24 hours.

6 • Make the sauce: Peel and halve the shallot. Roughly chop the chives. In the bowl of a food processor, combine the anchovies, capers, chives, shallots, and the remaining tarragon sprigs. Pulse to combine, then set aside.

7 • Just before serving, unwrap the calf's head and slice it as thinly as possible. Arrange the slices on a plate, drizzle with the sauce, and top with arugula, chanterelles, and julienned radish, if desired.

Bistrot
Paul Bert
PAUL BERT

BISTROT
PAUL

POIREAUX VINAIGRETTE

AU LARD CROUSTILLANT

(Leeks Vinaigrette with Crispy Bacon)

Serves 2

Preparation time: 10 minutes
Cooking time: 17 minutes
Resting time: 30 minutes

---

6 leeks (as thin as you can find)
4 chives
4 slices bacon
Salt and freshly ground black pepper
1 cup (250 ml) Vinaigrette *(page 210)*
2 sprigs flat-leaf parsley
Julienned radish

1 • Preheat the oven to 350°F (180°C).

2 • Trim off the rough upper ends of the leek greens and the bottom root end. Peel off the outer layer of leaves, then cut them into pieces about 4 inches (10 cm) long and rinse the leeks under cold running water. Pat them dry and set aside. Rinse the chives under a slow stream of cold water. Thoroughly pat them dry using a paper towel, then finely chop them.

3 • Bring a pot of water to a boil. Add the leeks and cook for 7 minutes until bright green and tender. Immediately transfer the leeks to a bowl of ice water to stop the cooking and maintain their color. Drain and set aside.

4 • Arrange the bacon slices on a baking sheet lined with parchment paper. Cover the slices with a piece of parchment paper, then place a baking sheet on top to help keep the slices from curling up while baking. Bake for 10 minutes until crisp. Let cool for 30 minutes at room temperature.

5 • Evenly divide the leeks between 2 serving plates. Season with salt and pepper. Spoon the vinaigrette over the top and sprinkle with the chives. Place 2 pieces of bacon on each plate and top with a parsley sprig and julienned radish.

LE BISTROT
PAUL BERT
Paris

PAUL BERT

TERRINE DE CAMPAGNE

(Country-Style Terrine)

Serves about 8

(using a 2-quart [1.8-liter] terrine mold)
Preparation time: 30 minutes
Cooking time: 1½ hours
Resting time: 3 days 15 minutes

---

6 shallots
2 cloves garlic
5 sprigs thyme
1 pound 2 ounces (500 g) pork liver
1 pound 2 ounces (500 g) chicken liver
4½ pounds (2 kg) pork neck
1 cup (250 ml) heavy cream
3 tablespoons cognac
2 large (100 g) eggs
5¾ teaspoons salt
3½ teaspoons freshly ground black pepper

1 • Preheat the oven to 350°F (180°C), or 340°F (170°C) for a convection oven.

2 • Peel and finely chop the shallots. Peel and halve the garlic cloves. Remove and discard any sprouts from the center of the cloves. Crush the garlic using the flat side of a knife blade. Remove the leaves from the thyme. Using a meat grinder, grind the pork and chicken livers and the pork neck. Place the ground meats in a large bowl. Add the cream, cognac, thyme leaves, shallots, garlic, eggs, salt, and pepper.

3 • While wearing a pair of food-grade gloves, mix the ground meats together using your hands until thoroughly combined. Place the mixture in the terrine mold. Place the terrine in a deep oven-safe baking dish and pour water into the dish about halfway up the terrine. Bake for 1½ hours, or until the internal temperature of the meat registers 176°F (80°C), when measured in the center with an instant-read thermometer.

4 • Remove the terrine from the oven. Wrap a weight (like a piece of cardboard or wood cut to the size of the mold with heavy objects like cans stacked on top) in plastic wrap and place it on top of the meat for 15 minutes to press it. Once the terrine has cooled completely, refrigerate it for 3 days before serving.

CÉLERI RÉMOULADE

(Celery Root in Remoulade Sauce)

erves 2

reparation time: 20 minutes

¼ medium celery root
½ bunch chervil (see Tip)
tablespoon Meaux mustard (or a coarse-grain Dijon mustard)
uice of ½ lemon
large egg yolk
alt and freshly ground black pepper
tablespoons (75 ml) peanut oil
herry vinegar
rugula, julienned radish, and olive oil (optional)

1 • Peel and coarsely grate the celery root. Transfer it to a large bowl of water and set aside. Rinse the chervil under a slow stream of cold water. Thoroughly dry it using a paper towel, then finely chop it.

2 • In a medium mixing bowl, combine the mustard, lemon juice, and egg yolk. Season with salt and pepper, then whisk until thoroughly combined.

3 • Add the oil in a thin drizzle while whisking as vigorously as possible, until a smooth mayonnaise consistency is achieved. Add a splash of sherry vinegar and the chopped chervil. Whisk to combine.

4 • Thoroughly drain the celery root, then transfer it to another medium mixing bowl. Add the chervil mayonnaise and stir to thoroughly coat.

5 • Spoon the mixture neatly into the center of each of 2 serving plates. Use a stainless-steel cooking ring, if desired, to create a more uniform appearance. Top with arugula and radish and a drizzle of olive oil, if desired.

Tip: If you can't find chervil, you can substitute with a bunch of your favorite fresh green herb or a combination of parsley and tarragon. Chervil is also an easy herb to grow.

PAUL

FRICASSÉE DE CHAMPIGNONS

(Mushrooms with Butter and Garlic)

Serves 2

Preparation time: 10 minutes
Cooking time: 10 minutes

12 ounces (350 g) seasonal mushrooms (oyster, golden chanterelles, porcini, etc.)
1 bunch curly parsley
2 cloves garlic
¼ cup (½ stick/60 g) unsalted butter
Salt and freshly ground black pepper

1 • Briefly rinse the mushrooms under cold running water. Thoroughly dry them, then wipe them with a clean towel to ensure all remaining impurities are removed. Rinse the parsley under a slow stream of cold water. Dry it using a paper towel, then finely chop it. Peel and halve the garlic cloves. Remove and discard any sprouts from the center of the cloves. Finely chop the garlic and set it aside.

2 • In a large skillet over high heat, melt the butter until very hot. Add the mushrooms and garlic. Cook, stirring frequently, to prevent sticking and burning, for 10 minutes, or just until golden. Season with salt and pepper just before serving. Sprinkle the parsley on top.

PAUL BERT

THE CREW

To tell the truth, I'm not a fan of the word "team," as it often suggests that there is an opposing force. I prefer "the crew," which embodies the idea of working in harmony with the environment rather than in opposition to it. A good crew knows when to reduce the sails if the wind picks up or to raise them during times of light breezes. Each member has their own place, function, personality, and talent.

There is no such thing as a bad crew member; some people just simply don't belong, or they have chosen to board the wrong vessel. For example, the head server of a two-Michelin-star restaurant—where welcoming customers is rooted in a sense of acceptance, or abdication even, linked to the establishment's reputation, the comfort of the table, and the quality of the dishes (often accompanied by high prices)—may not be suited to work as a head server in our bistros, as such a stuffy, and perhaps even mortifying, approach to dining often creates an atmosphere that feels out of touch with contemporary society—at least with the society I aspire to be a part of.

We are quite different from that. Thomas, who reigns behind the bar, acts as sommelier, cashier, and bartender, when necessary. He manages a wine list, assisted by Raphaël, containing more than five hundred labels, and he oversees a reservation book filled with chaotic highlights, pencil strokes, erasures, and names of all kinds—some with too many x's and not enough vowels—along with phone numbers that are often too long or incorrectly recorded. And let's not forget that incessant phone that rings nonstop on multiple lines! Nevertheless, we stay fully booked.

Thomas is calm and composed, almost saintly. He smiles at Nathalie, who stands in front of the bar with a look of dismay, balancing two plates on her left arm and holding a plate of fries for four in her right hand. "Dears, my Clos Rougeard 2015 for table 14, where is it?" There is also Olivier, Nicolas, and the other servers who rush back and forth from the terrace to the kitchen, clearing dishes while being scolded by the chef for accepting substitutions. They all have to deal with customers who don't understand why beef tartare isn't cooked or that asparagus has a season, which is why it isn't available in September even though they saw it on Instagram. Fortunately, most of our customers are delightful, understanding, and, above all, happy to be with us. They seek our attention, want to be photographed with Nathalie, return year after year, and send her kisses when they leave and greet Olivier when they arrive. All of this unfolds, service after service, in a joyful atmosphere that can become chaotic if someone at table number 8 spills a drink. In such cases, it's up to the server's skill to save the day. A quick change of tablecloth, a smile at the neighboring table to double-check they were not impacted, and a touch of humor restores everyone's happiness. To use another maritime phrase: "White on red, nothing moves!"*

*A popular saying that means that white wine should be drunk before red wine. In terms of sailing, a white flag over the red signals that the vessel should remain in port.

gel

PAUL BERT
LE BISTROT

OS À MOELLE

(Bone Marrow)

Serves 2

Preparation time: 5 minutes
Cooking time: 20 minutes

¼ red onion
clove garlic
2 sprigs chervil (see Tip, page 65)
2 chives
small baguette, cut widthwise into 2 4-inch (10 cm) sections
marrowbones, between 3 and 4 inches (8 and 10 cm) each (ask the butcher to cut them lengthwise in half)
Fleur de sel sea salt

1 • Preheat the oven to 350°F (180°C).

2 • Peel the onion and garlic. Rinse the chervil and chives under a slow stream of cold water. Thoroughly dry them. Finely chop the onion, chervil, and chives. Set aside.

3 • Cut the baguette sections lengthwise in half, then toast the halves for several minutes until golden. Rub the garlic on the toasted slices.

4 • Place the marrowbones in a baking dish. Season with sea salt, then bake for about 15 minutes (or a little more depending on the amount of marrow in the bone), until the marrow is softened. Then turn the oven broiler on and broil for 5 minutes, until lightly browned, but stop before the marrow turns to liquid.

5 • Arrange the marrowbones on each of 2 serving plates accompanied by 2 slices of toasted garlic bread on each plate. Sprinkle the red onion, chervil, and chives on each marrowbone and serve immediately.

TARTINE DE PAIN GRILLÉ

AU BEURRE SALÉ, VIEUX COMTÉ ET TRUFFE NOIRE

(Grilled Bread with Salted Butter, Aged Comté, and Black Truffle)

Serves 2

Preparation time: 5 minutes
Cooking time: 5 minutes
Resting time: 5 minutes

1½ ounces (40 g) black truffles
1½ ounces (40 g) 24-month-aged Comté cheese
¼ large baguette
2 tablespoons salted butter, softened

1 • Very thinly shave the truffles, preferably using a mandoline. Thinly slice the Comté into large shavings.

2 • Cut the baguette lengthwise in half. Toast each half, then set aside for 5 minutes at room temperature.

3 • Spread 1 tablespoon of salted butter on each toasted baguette half, then place the slices of Comté on top, and top with the truffle shavings. Serve immediately.

Tip: Replace the Comté cheese with foie gras, if desired.

CROQUE À LA TRUFFE

(Grilled Comté, Ham, and Truffle Sandwich)

erves 2

reparation time: 10 minutes
esting time: 2 days
ooking time: 5 minutes (béchamel) plus 6 minutes (sandwich)

---

or the Béchamel

½ tablespoons unsalted butter
tablespoons all-purpose flour
cup (250 ml) whole milk
/hole nutmeg

½ ounces (40 g) black truffles
½ ounces (40 g) 12-month-aged Comté cheese
½ tablespoons unsalted butter, softened
slices white sandwich bread
thin slices Prince de Paris jambon blanc or another superior-quality cooked ham
alt and freshly ground black pepper
alad greens dressed with Vinaigrette *(page 210)*, **for serving**

1 • Make the béchamel: In a medium saucepan over low heat, melt the butter. Add the flour and combine to make a roux. Place over medium heat and cook for about 2 minutes, but without browning (this makes a white roux). While stirring continuously using a whisk, add the milk to the roux a little at a time until incorporated and the mixture is thickened and smooth. Turn off the heat and grate a little nutmeg into the mixture.

2 • Very thinly slice the truffles and Comté, preferably using a mandoline. Set aside.

3 • Spread the softened butter on both sides of the bread slices. Assemble the sandwiches as follows: Place one slice of sandwich bread on a work surface and spread a thin layer of béchamel on top. Add a few slices of Comté, a slice of ham, and a few slices of truffle. Top with the second slice of bread.

4 • Wrap each sandwich in plastic wrap and refrigerate for 48 hours. This will give the aroma of the fresh truffle time to infuse into the béchamel.

5 • In a large skillet, panfry each sandwich over high heat for 3 minutes on each side. There is no need to grease the skillet since the bread has butter on the outside. Serve with a green salad.

CROUSTILLANT DE PIED DE COCHON

(Breaded Pig's Foot)

Serves 4

(using a 2-quart [1.8-liter] terrine mold)
Preparation time: 15 minutes
Cooking time: 3½ hours
Resting time: 24 hours

---

2 carrots
1 yellow onion
1 clove garlic
1 small stalk celery
1 clove
2 sprigs thyme
1 bay leaf
4 pig's feet
2 shallots
½ bunch tarragon
Salt and freshly ground black pepper
3 tablespoons all-purpose flour
¼ cup (25 g) dried breadcrumbs
2 large (100 g) eggs
Peanut oil
3½ tablespoons (50 g) unsalted butter
Chives, finely chopped

---

1 • The day before serving, peel 1 carrot, the onion, and garlic. Cut the onion in half. Bring a large pot of water to a boil. Place the onion halves, peeled carrot, garlic, celery, clove, thyme, bay leaf, and pig's feet in the boiling water. After several minutes, skim off any impurities from the surface of the water. Cook, uncovered, over low heat for 3 hours, until the pig's feet are very tender.

2 • At the end of the cooking time, remove the pig's feet and remove the meat and discard the bones.

3 • In a medium saucepan over medium heat, bring 4 cups (1 L) of the broth from the pot to a simmer. Simmer, uncovered, for about 30 minutes to reduce, then strain.

4 • Peel and finely dice the remaining carrot into very small cubes. Peel and finely chop the shallots. Rinse the tarragon under a slow stream of cold water. Thoroughly pat it dry using a paper towel, then finely chop it.

5 • Add the diced carrot, shallots, tarragon, and flesh from the pig's feet to the reduced juice. Season with salt and pepper. Transfer the mixture to a terrine and refrigerate for 24 hours.

6 • The next day, unmold the mixture and cut it int slices approximately 1 inch (3 cm) thick. Add the flour, bread crumbs, and eggs to 3 separate shallo bowls. Lightly beat the eggs using a fork. Dredge each slice to fully coat them in this order: the flour, then the beaten eggs, then the bread crumbs. Dredge each slice two more times. Season again with salt and pepper.

7 • In a large skillet over medium heat, heat a generous drizzle of oil. Add the butter and let melt. Add the breaded pig's feet slices and cook for about 4 minutes on each side, until golden brown. Sprinkle with finely chopped chives to serve.

Tip: At the restaurant, we serve this dish with Tart Sauce (page 212) and a green salad on the side.

PAUL BERT
Paris
PAUL BERT

PAUL BERT

SALADE VERTE AU COMTÉ

ET À LA TRUFFE

(Green Salad with Comté and Black Truffle)

Serves 2

Preparation time: 10 minutes

1½ ounces (40 g) black truffles
1½ ounces (40 g) 24-month-aged Comté cheese
7 ounces (200 g) salad greens
⅔ cup (150 ml) Vinaigrette *(page 210)*
Salt and freshly ground black pepper
Julienned radish

1 • Very thinly shave the truffles, preferably using a mandoline. Thinly slice the Comté into large shavings.

2 • Wash and thoroughly dry the salad greens, then transfer them to a large mixing bowl. Add the vinaigrette. Season with salt and pepper. Toss the greens with the vinaigrette to evenly coat them.

3 • Arrange the salad in serving bowls. Place a few shavings of Comté and truffle and julienned radish on top. Serve.

SALADE FRISÉE AUX LARDONS

PISSENLIT SAUVAGE ET OEUF MOLLET

(Curly Endive Salad with Lardons, Dandelion Greens, and Poached Eggs)

Serves 2

Preparation time: 10 minutes
Cooking time: 15 minutes

1¾ ounces (50 g) curly endive
1¾ ounces (50 g) dandelion greens
2 slices bacon
3 tablespoons sherry vinegar
2 heaping tablespoons crème fraîche
2 large organic eggs
⅔ cup (150 ml) distilled white vinegar
Freshly ground black pepper

---

1 • Rinse the endive and dandelion under cold running water. Thoroughly pat them dry using paper towels. Set aside.

2 • Cut the bacon slices into small pieces. In a medium skillet over medium heat, fry the bacon for 5 minutes, or until golden brown. Transfer to a paper towel–lined plate to drain completely. Deglaze the hot pan with the sherry vinegar. Add the crème fraîche to the pan, reduce the heat to low, and stir until the crème fraîche has melted. Once the sauce is smooth, set aside off the heat.

3 • Break each egg into its own small ramekin. Bring a saucepan of water to a boil. Add the white vinegar. As soon as the water is boiling, stir it with a wooden spoon in a clockwise direction to create a gentle swirl. When the water is swirling, hold the ramekins just above the surface of the water and gently pour in the eggs. Cook for 4 minutes, until the whites are set and the yolks are at your desired doneness. Remove them using a slotted spoon and transfer to a paper towel–lined plate to drain completely.

4 • Place the endive and dandelion in a mixing bowl. Add the warm crème fraîche mixture and toss to completely coat the salad. Taste, and season with pepper, if desired. Adding the warm sauce to the lettuce and dandelion will help soften their fibers so that they wilt without having to cook them.

5 • Arrange the salad on 2 serving plates, then place a poached egg on each plate.

OEUFS MIMOSA

(Deviled Eggs)

erves 2

reparation time: 5 minutes
ooking time: 9 minutes

medium organic eggs
⅓ cup (80 g) Mayonnaise *(page 211)*

1 • Bring a saucepan of water to a boil. Add the eggs and cook for 9 minutes. Transfer the eggs to a strainer and place them under cold running water to immediately stop the cooking.

2 • Peel the eggs, then cut them in half. Remove the yolks and place them in a mixing bowl. Set the cooked egg white halves aside.

3 • Add the mayonnaise to the cooked egg yolks and mix using a fork until smooth.

4 • Fill the egg white halves with the mixture. Arrange the halves in groups of 4 on each of 2 serving plates.

Tip: Just as with *Oeufs Mayonnaise* (page 32), you can flavor the mayonnaise and cooked egg yolk mixture according to the season: with truffle, finely chopped wild garlic, bottarga, or taramasalata topped with salmon roe.

ASPERGES BLANCHES VINAIGRETTE

ET OEUF MOLLET

(White Asparagus Vinaigrette and Soft-Boiled Egg)

Serves 2

Preparation time: 5 minutes
Cooking time: 3 to 5 minutes (asparagus) plus 4½ minutes (egg)
Resting time: 2 to 3 minutes

---

6 spears white asparagus
4 chives
Salt
2 large organic eggs
Just over ¾ cup (200 ml) Vinaigrette *(page 210)*

1 • Peel the asparagus. Rinse the chives under a slow stream of cold water. Thoroughly dry them using a paper towel, then finely chop them. Bring a large saucepan of salted water to a boil. Add the asparagus and cook for 3 to 5 minutes, depending on their diameter, maintaining the water at a boil. Test for doneness using the tip of a knife. If the asparagus still feels a little firm, cook for a few more minutes. Once cooked, drain, then thoroughly pat them dry using a paper towel.

2 • Bring a separate pan of water to a boil. Add the eggs to the boiling water and cook for 4½ minutes. Once cooked, immediately remove the eggs from the water and place them under cold running water for 2 to 3 minutes to immediately stop the cooking. Peel the eggs and set them aside until ready to serve.

3 • Arrange 3 asparagus spears on each of 2 serving plates. Drizzle the asparagus with some of the vinaigrette, top with a soft-boiled egg, and sprinkle with chives.

Mauviel

PAUL BERT

JOUES DE LOTTE

EN TEMPURA

(Monkfish Cheek Tempura)

erves 2

reparation time: 5 minutes
ooking time: 5 to 6 minutes

eanut oil, for deep frying
large (50 g) egg
cups (250 g) panko breadcrumbs
4 ounces (400 g) monkfish cheeks (or use scallops or a firm white fish such as cod or halibut cut into chunks)

1 • Preheat a deep fryer or large heavy pot with peanut oil to 350°F (180°C).

2 • In a small bowl, lightly beat the egg using a fork. Add the breadcrumbs to a separate bowl. Dredge the monkfish cheeks one by one (so that they do not stick together) in the egg, then in the breadcrumbs to fully coat them.

3 • Place the cheeks into the hot oil and fry for 5 to 6 minutes, until crisp and golden. Pat them using a paper towel to remove excess oil.

Tip: In the restaurant, we serve monkfish cheek tempura with Tartar Sauce (page 212), a lemon wedge, and finely chopped chives.

SALADE DE LENDEMAIN DE POT-AU-FEU

(Next-Day Pot-au-Feu Salad)

Serves 2

Preparation time: 10 minutes
Cooking time: 15 minutes

2 sprigs chervil (see Tip, page 65)
½ red onion
2 carrots
1 pound 2 ounces (500 g) cooked beef (left over from the previous day's pot-au-feu, see Tip)
2 boiled yellow fingerling potatoes (left over from the previous day's pot-au-feu)
⅔ cup (150 ml) Vinaigrette *(page 210)*
Salt and freshly ground black pepper

1 • Rinse the chervil under a slow stream of cold water. Thoroughly pat it dry using paper towels, then finely chop it. Peel and thinly slice the onion. Peel the carrots, then cut them into small cubes.

2 • Bring a saucepan of water to a boil and add the carrots. Cook over medium heat for about 10 minutes, until very tender when pierced with a fork. Drain, then set aside.

3 • Cut the cold meat and potatoes into medium cubes.

4 • Transfer the cubes of meat, carrots, and potatoes to a mixing bowl. Season with salt and pepper. Add the vinaigrette and stir to evenly coat.

5 • Neatly arrange the salad on 2 serving plates. Top with the sliced onion and a sprinkle of chervil.

Tip: Any leftover cooked potato or cooked meat such as from a pot roast or beef stew could work fo this dish.

PAUL BERT

LE BISTROT
PAUL BERT

SALADE DE CHAMPIGNONS DE PARIS

CRÈME ET CIBOULETTE

(White Button Mushroom Salad, Cream, and Chives)

Serves 2

Preparation time: 15 minutes

---

4 ounces (400 g) white button mushrooms
chives
⅔ cup (150 ml) heavy cream
Juice of 1 lemon
Salt and freshly ground black pepper

1 • Briefly rinse the mushrooms under cold running water and cut off the rough ends from their stems. Quarter the mushrooms. Rinse the chives under a slow stream of cold water. Thoroughly dry them using a paper towel, then finely chop them.

2 • In a mixing bowl, combine the cream and lemon juice. Whisk until smooth. Add the mushrooms and most of the chopped chives to the bowl and stir to evenly coat. Season with salt and pepper.

3 • Neatly arrange the salad on 2 serving plates and garnish with the remaining chives.

FROMAGE DE TÊTE

(Head Cheese)

Serves 5

Preparation time: 20 minutes
Cooking time: 2 hours 40 minutes
Resting time: 48 hours

---

5 quarts (5 L) water
1 pound (450 g) curing salt (or purchase sodium nitrate online)
¼ cup (50 g) sugar
4 heads suckling pig
2 calf's feet
6 shallots
2 cloves garlic
½ bunch flat-leaf parsley
½ bunch tarragon
Just over ¾ cup (200 ml) vinegar
Salt and freshly ground black pepper

For the Stock Aromatics

2 carrots
2 onions
2 cloves
1 stalk celery
2 bay leaves
2 sprigs thyme
1 teaspoon peppercorns

---

1 • Pour the water into a large mixing bowl. Add the curing salt and sugar. Add the heads and refrigerate for 24 hours.

2 • The next day, make the aromatic stock: Peel the carrots and onions. Rinse the heads and calf's feet under running water, then pat them dry with a clean cloth.

3 • Bring a large stockpot of water to a boil. Add the carrots, onions, cloves, celery, bay leaves, thyme, and peppercorns.

4 • Add the heads and feet to the pot, ensuring they are completely covered with water.

5 • Cook for 2½ hours uncovered over low heat, until the heads and feet are very tender. Remove the flesh (fat and lean meat) from the bones and place it in a large bowl.

6 • Strain half the cooking liquid. In a saucepan over high heat, reduce the broth by about one-fourth.

7 • Peel the shallots and garlic cloves. Remove and discard any sprouts from the center of the cloves. Crush the garlic using the flat side of a knife blade. Rinse the parsley and tarragon under a slow stream of cold water. Thoroughly dry them using paper towels, then finely chop them. Finely chop the shallots. Place the shallots, garlic, parsley, and tarragon in a large bowl.

8 • In a separate saucepan, bring the vinegar to a boil. As soon as the vinegar is boiling, pour it into the bowl with the shallots, garlic, and herbs. Add the reduced cooking liquid. Season with salt and pepper, if necessary. Stir the mixture to thoroughly combine.

9 • Arrange the meat from the heads in a terrine, creating layers by alternating lean meat with the fat pieces. Pour the broth mixture into the terrine over the meat.

10 • Refrigerate for 24 hours before serving.

(MAINS)

ATS

CARPACCIO DE BOEUF

(Beef Carpaccio)

Serves 2

Preparation time: 20 minutes

---

7 ounces (200 g) assorted beef pieces (tenderloin, strip steak, top round, eye of round)
4 white button mushrooms
2 cups (50 g) arugula
6 leaves basil
2 chives
¾ ounce (20 g) Parmesan cheese
1 tablespoon capers (see Tip)
Olive oil
Fleur de sel sea salt

1 • Ask your butcher to very thinly slice the beef pieces. Briefly rinse the mushrooms under cold running water and cut off the rough ends from their stems. Rinse the arugula and basil leaves under a slow stream of cold water. Thoroughly pat them dry using paper towels.

2 • Rinse the chives under a slow stream of cold water. Thoroughly pat them dry using a paper towel then finely chop them. Peel the mushroom tops, then thinly slice the mushrooms. Roughly tear the basil leaves. Thinly shave the Parmesan. Drain the capers, then roughly chop. Set aside.

3 • Neatly arrange the slices of beef on 2 serving plates. Arrange a few arugula leaves and mushroom slices on top. Add pieces of basil.

4 • Drizzle oil over the top. Add a pinch of sea salt, the chopped capers, Parmesan shavings, and the chopped chives.

Tip: Try to find salted capers, which are much better than those in brine, and should be rinsed and drained before use. The best ones come from Salina.

LE BISTROT
PAUL BERT

LE BISTROT
PAUL BERT

TARTARE DE BOEUF

(Beef Tartare)

erves 2

reparation time: 10 minutes

- shallots
- ½ bunch flat-leaf parsley
- ½ bunch chives
- teaspoon capers
- 2¾ ounces (360 g) ground beef (preferably skirt steak or rump steak)
- alt and freshly ground black pepper
- teaspoons mild mustard, plus more for serving
- abasco sauce (optional)
- live oil

1 • Peel and finely chop the shallots. Rinse the parsley and chives under a slow stream of cold water. Thoroughly pat them dry, then finely chop them. Roughly chop the capers.

2 • Place the ground beef in a large bowl. Add the capers, shallots, parsley, and chives. Season with salt and pepper. Add the mustard, Tabasco, if using, and a light drizzle of oil. Thoroughly combine the mixture.

3 • Neatly arrange the beef mixture on 2 serving plates using a stainless-steel cooking ring, top with a small spoonful of mustard, and serve immediately.

Tip: Alternatively, you can panfry the beef mixture for a few minutes on each side; it's delicious this way, too. This dish is a timeless icon of our restaurant, honoring simplicity by only lightly seasoning it to preserve the meat's natural flavor. We also do not add egg yolk, to prevent the meat from clumping together. We almost always serve beef tartare topped with a little Dijon mustard and fries (page 199) on the side.

LE BISTROT
PAUL BERT

SAINT-JACQUES RÔTIES ENTIÈRES

AU KARI GOSSE

(Whole Roasted Scallops in Kari Gosse Butter)

Serves 2

Preparation time: 10 minutes
Cooking time: 3 minutes

---

6 scallops in the shell
7 tablespoons (100 g) unsalted butter, softened
Kari Gosse (a proprietary spice mixture from Brittany made of ginger, chile, black pepper, cloves, cinnamon, and turmeric; order online, or substitute with your own spice blend)
Salt and freshly ground black pepper

1 • Preheat the oven to 400°F (200°C).

2 • Clean the scallops, taking care not to detach the flesh from the shells. Remove the frill, gut, and coral (the orange tongue-shaped sac). Rinse and pat dry. Freeze the coral, if desired, for other uses, such as in sauces. Season the softened butter with Kari Gosse, then thoroughly combine to a smooth consistency.

3 • Place about 1 tablespoon of the Kari Gosse butter on top of each scallop. Bake for about 3 minutes, until the butter is bubbling, and the scallop is just starting to brown. Season with salt and pepper and serve immediately.

Tip: We serve scallops at the bistro accompanied by haricots Coco de Paimpol (a white bean from Brittany) or chanterelles, depending on the season.

PAUL BERT'S FIRST CHEF, SÉBASTIEN ALESSANDRI

The beginnings of the bistro were erratic. We opened with Sébastien Alessandri as our chef, a talented self-taught cook. In the 1980s, he ran the kitchens at Le Cabanon du Maître Nageur, where both servers and cooks wore kimonos! First and foremost, he was my friend. He was young, handsome, and adventurous. He was Corsican, a hunter and storyteller, often sharing tales from his homeland of hunting, chestnuts, aromas, and the maquis. But most importantly, he was a tireless cook. We were supposed to become partners, but on the day we were going to sign the paperwork, before entering the attorney's office, he invited me to have coffee at a bistro whose name, address, and existence I have forgotten. He unassumingly mentioned, "You'll have to sign without me. I've got cancer, but don't worry, I'm not letting you down. I'll take care of the cooking. I'll make bisque!"

We didn't dwell on it; that would not have suited him. The agreement lasted a year. It was wonderful, extraordinary, and complete sadness. It ended in a cold hospital room where I came to say goodbye. His eyes were bright, and he maintained clarity of mind. I didn't know what to say. With my mind in a jumble, I stammered the first thing that came to mind: "The weather is fine. It's the opening of the hunting season." I took his hand, and in one breath, he said, "Today, I am the rabbit." He had a real talent for killer phrases. A few weeks earlier, when he had fled Paris to hide away in Cargèse while living with me, I had yelled at him on the phone for forgetting to come home for his chemotherapy. He retorted, "Forget it. The weather is great. I want to watch the sunset, then jump in the car and drive behind the hill. I'll get to see it sink below the horizon and disappear into the sea. With the time I have left, I can't deny myself two sunsets a day. So, you know what you can do with your chemo!"

The bistro had been open just a year when Johnny joined us. He was the former chef of my first bistro, Les Voyageurs, on rue Keller. The customers came and time passed. Weeks turned to months. Johnny eventually left, and our search for a new chef began. We endured two years of challenges, during which chefs came and went—some good, some average, some one-of-a-kind, while others were bad, annoying, dishonest, or drank too much. We held on, and then Thierry arrived.

AILE DE RAIE AUX CÂPRES

(Skate Wing with Capers)

erves 2

eparation time: 10 minutes
oking time: 13 minutes

- bunch chervil (see Tip, page 65)
- slice white sandwich bread, crust removed
- lemon
- eutral-flavor oil
- pieces skate wing (about 7 ounces/200 g each)
- alt and freshly ground black pepper
- tablespoon capers
- ½ tablespoons unsalted butter

1 • Rinse the chervil under a slow stream of cold water. Thoroughly pat it dry using paper towels, then roughly chop it. Cut the bread into small cubes. Wash the lemon and cut it into small cubes, including the peel. Set aside.

2 • In a medium skillet, heat a drizzle of oil over high heat. Add the sandwich bread cubes and cook for 4 or 5 minutes, until golden brown. Transfer to a paper towel–lined plate to drain.

3 • Season the skate wings with salt and pepper. Place a skillet over high heat and add the butter and a drizzle of oil. Cook the wings for about 4 minutes on each side while continually basting them with the oil and butter from the pan. Add the capers, half the chervil, and the lemon.

4 • Just before serving, add the croutons and remaining chervil.

Tip: Serve the skate with Boiled Potatoes (page 206).

LANGUE DE BOEUF SAUCE PIQUANTE

(Beef Tongue with Piquant Sauce)

Serves 2

Preparation time: 10 minutes
Cooking time: 3 hours

6 cups (1.5 L) beef stock
1 beef tongue (about 14 ounces/400 g)
1 teaspoon kosher salt
1 teaspoon peppercorns
1 bouquet garni (see Tip, page 38)
6 very ripe tomatoes
2 red chiles (such as Thai bird's eye, Fresno, or cayenne)
6 cornichons (see Tip)
Salt and freshly ground black pepper

1 • Pour the stock into a large pot. Add the beef tongue, kosher salt, peppercorns, and bouquet garni. Bring to a boil over high heat, then skim off any impurities and the foam from the surface. Reduce the heat to low and cook for 2½ hours with the lid askew. When the tongue is tender and the skin will easily peel off, remove it from the pot and set it aside to drain. Peel off the slightly firm skin from the surface. Cut the tongue into slices and set them aside.

2 • Simmer the broth over high heat for 15 minutes to reduce it by about one-third. Peel the tomatoes and remove the stems. Add the tomatoes to the reduced cooking broth. Add the chile. Cook for 5 minutes, then blend using an immersion blender until smooth.

3 • Slice the cornichons into rounds. Arrange the tongue slices on 2 serving plates. Coat with the sauce, top with the sliced cornichons, season with salt and pepper, and serve.

Tip: At the restaurant, we serve beef tongue with Puréed Potatoes (page 204). To make the recipe even more delicious, we use Malossol cornichons. Their vinegary, sweet flavor balances the spiciness of the sauce.

LE BIS

BLANQUETTE DE VEAU

(Veal in White Sauce)

erves 2 to 4

reparation time: 10 minutes
ooking time: 3½ hours

0½ ounces (300 g) veal shoulder
0½ ounces (300 g) veal foreribs
carrots
bunch grelot onions (or use 5 or 6 pearl onions)
ounces (200 g) white button mushrooms
cups (1 L) water
alt and freshly ground black pepper
bouquet garni (see Tip, page 38)
cups (1 L) heavy cream
large (60 g) egg yolks
uice of 2 lemons
hopped fresh herbs

1 • Cut the meat into medium pieces.

2 • Peel the carrots and onions. Cut the carrots into large pieces. Briefly rinse the mushrooms under cold running water and cut off the rough ends from their stems. Quarter the mushrooms.

3 • In a large pot, add 4 cups (1 L) of salted water and some black pepper. Bring to a boil. Add the meat pieces and the bouquet garni and cook, covered, for 2½ hours, until the meat is tender. Drain the meat and set aside off the heat.

4 • Strain the cooking liquid and add it to a saucepan. Add the mushrooms and 3¾ cups (900 ml) of the cream. In a small bowl, beat the yolks with the remaining cream, then add this to the cooking liquid mixture and stir to gently combine. Cook for about 30 minutes over low heat to reduce.

5 • Add the veal meat, carrots, and onions. Cook for 30 minutes over medium heat.

6 • Add the lemon juice at the end of the cooking time and adjust the seasoning as needed. Garnish with chopped herbs before serving.

vice
Ext. N°

UISINE

FRICASSÉE DE TÊTE DE SEICHE

ET FREGOLA SARDA

(Cuttlefish and Fregola Sarda)

Serves 2

Preparation time: 20 minutes
Cooking time: 1 hour 50 minutes

---

14 ounces (400 g) cuttlefish heads
1 bunch cilantro
1 onion
½ bunch chervil (see Tip, page 65)
1 preserved lemon
1 bouquet garni (see Tip, page 38)
Olive oil
Salt and freshly ground black pepper
7 ounces (200 g) fregola sarda
Scant ½ cup (100 ml) dry white wine
2 tablespoons crushed tomatoes

1 • Thoroughly clean the cuttlefish heads under cold running water, then thoroughly pat them dry using paper towels. Rinse the cilantro under a slow stream of cold water. Thoroughly pat it dry, then chop it. Peel the onion and finely chop it. Finely chop the chervil. Cut the preserved lemon into very small cubes.

2 • Bring a pot of water to a boil. Add the cuttlefish heads and bouquet garni and cook, covered, over low heat for 1½ hours, until the cuttlefish is opaque and tender. Drain and set aside.

3 • In a hot skillet, heat a generous drizzle of oil over high heat. Add the cuttlefish heads. Season with salt and pepper. Cook the heads for about 5 minutes to brown them. Add the lemon and cilantro. Stir to combine. Set aside off the heat.

4 • Heat a drizzle of oil in a medium saucepan over medium heat. Add the onion and cook until browned. Add the fregola and cook for 3 minutes, until well coated in oil and heated through. Deglaze the pan with the wine. Add just enough water to cover the ingredients, then add the tomatoes. Stir to combine and cook, stirring constantly, over low heat for 10 minutes, until the liquid is absorbed and the fregola is al dente.

5 • Arrange the fregola sarda on 2 serving plates using a stainless-steel cooking ring. Arrange the cuttlefish heads on the fregola and serve.

Paul Bert

RIS DE VEAU POÊLÉS

ET POMMES DE TERRE À L'ANGLAISE

(Panfried Sweetbreads and Boiled Potatoes)

Serves 2

Preparation time: about 11 minutes

---

2 sweetbreads (about 7 ounces/200 g each)
5 tablespoons (70 g) unsalted butter
Chopped fresh herbs
1 recipe Boiled Potatoes
(page 206)

1 • Ask the butcher to remove the thin membrane from the sweetbreads or remove it using a knife.

2 • In a large skillet over high heat, melt the butter. When the butter has completely melted and is foaming slightly, add the sweetbreads. Cook until golden brown on both sides, turning occasionally, then reduce the heat and finish cooking over low heat for an additional 6 minutes. While the sweetbreads are cooking, baste them continuously in the fat from the pan using a spoon. This will help ensure they cook evenly and are golden brown all over.

3 • Garnish with herbs and serve with boiled potatoes.

ALOYAU DE BOEUF SAUCE AU POIVRE

ET POMMES DE TERRE SAUTÉES

(Beef Sirloin, Peppercorn Sauce, and Sautéed Potatoes)

Serves 2

Preparation time: 6 minutes
Cooking time: 20 minutes

---

1 top sirloin steak (about 14 ounces/400 g), at room temperature
Salt and freshly ground black pepper
1½ tablespoons unsalted butter
Neutral-flavor oil
3 tablespoons Armagnac
Scant 1 cup (200 ml) crème fraîche
3½ tablespoons (25 g) cracked black peppercorns (preferably Sarawak)
Scant ½ cup (100 ml) heavy cream (optional, but recommended)
2 sprigs chervil (see Tip, page 65)
1 recipe Sautéed Potatoes *(page 207)*

1 • Season the sirloin with salt and pepper. Place a large skillet over high heat. Add the butter and a drizzle of oil. Add the sirloin and sear it for about 3 minutes on each side.

2 • When cooked to the desired temperature, remove the sirloin from the pan and let rest for several minutes on a plate while preparing the sauce.

3 • Deglaze the pan with the Armagnac. Light the Armagnac with a long match and reduce the heat to low. Stir in the crème fraîche, peppercorns, and a little of the heavy cream, if using. Cook for 5 minutes, or until the sauce thickens to a coating consistency. If the sauce looks separated, add a little more of the cream as needed until the sauce becomes smooth again when stirred, or add more cream to taste.

4 • Rinse the chervil under a slow stream of cold water. Thoroughly pat it dry, then chop it.

5 • Slice the sirloin and arrange it in a serving dish Top with the peppercorn sauce and sprinkle the chervil over the top. Serve with sauteed potatoes.

Tip: For a sirloin, there are only three cooking temperatures: very rare (2 minutes cooking time on each side), rare (the recommended temperature for this recipe), or poorly cooked!

LE BISTROT
PAUL BERT

CONFIT DE CANARD

ET POMMES SAUTÉES

(Duck Confit and Sautéed Apples)

Serves 2

Preparation time: 5 minutes
Cooking time: 3 hours
Resting time: 24 hours minimum

---

2 duck legs
5½ tablespoons (100 g) coarse kosher salt
Pinch freshly cracked peppercorns
7 ounces (200 g) duck fat

1 • Season the duck legs with the salt and some pepper on the flesh side, then wrap the legs in plastic wrap and refrigerate for 24 hours.

2 • Remove any excess salt and pepper from the legs. Place the duck fat in a Dutch oven and heat over medium heat. Add the legs. Reduce the heat to low and cook, covered, for 3 hours, until the meat is very tender and easily pulls away from the bone. Set aside to cool.

3 • To ensure a crisp skin, fry the legs (skin-side down) for several minutes in a hot skillet with a little duck fat and serve.

Tip: At the restaurant, we often serve the duck with sautéed apples (see page 152 for one way to make these).

2 Poulet
2 Soles

POULET

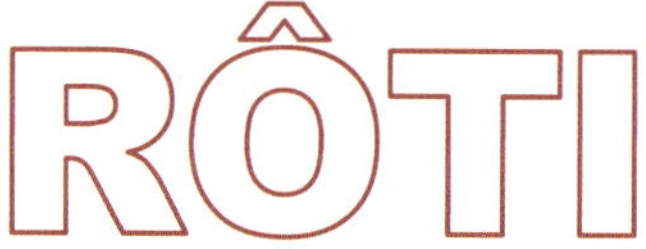

(*Roast Chicken*)

Serves 4

Preparation time: 10 minutes
Cooking time: 1 hour 45 minutes

½ bunch chervil (see Tip, page 65)
½ bunch chives
1 whole chicken (about 3⅓ pounds/1.5 kg)
1 tablespoon crème fraîche
1 bay leaf
7 tablespoons (100 g) unsalted butter, softened
Salt and freshly ground black pepper
1 recipe Fries *(page 199)*

1 • Preheat the oven to 350°F (180°C).

2 • Rinse the chervil and chives under a slow stream of cold water. Thoroughly pat them dry usin paper towels.

3 • Place the chicken in a baking dish. Add the crème fraîche, chervil, chives, and bay leaf to the inside of the chicken. Coat the outside of the chicken completely with the butter. Season with salt and pepper. Bake for 1 hour and 45 minutes. Check for doneness by making a slight incision at the top of the thigh. If the meat seems too pink or if the juices from the meat are not clear, bake for an additional 15 minutes. Serve the chicken with some of the juices from cooking and fries.

PARMENTIER DE BOEUF

(Beef Shepherd's Pie)

erves 2

reparation time: 10 minutes
ooking time: 35 minutes

- **2 bunch chervil (see Tip, page 65)**
- **shallot**
- **clove garlic**
- **tablespoon unsalted butter**
- **ounces (250 g) ground beef**
- **cant ½ cup (100 g) tomato sauce**
- **alt and freshly ground black pepper**
- **small sprigs lemon thyme**
- **recipe Pureed Potatoes** *(page 204)*
- **4 cup (25 g) dried breadcrumbs**
- **eutral-flavor oil**

1 • Preheat the oven to 350°F (180°C).

2 • Rinse the chervil under a slow stream of cold water. Thoroughly pat it dry using paper towels. Peel the shallot. Finely chop the chervil and shallot. Peel and halve the garlic clove. Remove and discard any green sprout from the center of the clove. Crush the garlic using the flat side of a knife blade and mince it.

3 • In a large skillet over high heat, melt the butter. Reduce the heat to medium, then add the shallot and garlic and cook for a minute or two, until light golden. Add the ground beef and tomato sauce and season with salt and pepper. Cook, stirring to break up the beef, for about 10 minutes, until the beef is cooked through. Add the thyme, then remove the pan from the heat.

4 • Arrange the meat mixture in small individual ramekins (2 6-inch-wide, 1-inch-deep [15.25 cm x 2.5 cm] baking dishes or 8-ounce/236 ml mini cocottes work well). Add the pureed potatoes to the top and spread them out evenly. Add a drizzle of oil on top and top with the breadcrumbs. Place on a baking sheet to catch any drips and bake for 25 minutes, or until bubbly and the potatoes are lightly browned. Garnish with chervil and serve.

Tip: We often like to add a thin layer of potato puree at the bottom of the ramekins too.

LE BISTROT
PAUL BERT

CUISINE

FOIE DE VEAU POÊLÉ

ET POMMES DE TERRE À L'ANGLAISE

(Panfried Calf's Liver and Boiled Potatoes)

erves 2

ooking time: 6 minutes

½ tablespoons (50 g) unsalted butter

veal liver cutlets (about 7 ounces/200 g each; ask your butcher for ones that are light in color)

ounces (200 g) Boiled Potatoes *(page 206)*

1 • In a large skillet, melt the butter over low heat. When the butter is foaming slightly, add the livers. Cook for 3 minutes on each side, until lightly browned.

2 • Serve with the boiled potatoes.

CARRÉ D'AGNEAU 4 CÔTES

ARTICHAUTS POIVRADE ET OLIVES NOIRES

(Rack of Lamb 4 Chops, Artichoke Poivrade, and Black Olives)

Serves 2

Preparation time: 15 minutes
Cooking time: 25 minutes

---

4 small purple artichokes
3½ tablespoons (50 g) unsalted butter
Juice of 1 lemon
1 rack of lamb (4 chops)
Salt and freshly ground black pepper
Neutral-flavor oil
1 cup (150 g) black olives

1 • Preheat the oven to 350°F (180°C).

2 • Trim the artichokes by removing all of the tough outer leaves to reveal the pale, tender center. Using a sharp paring knife, cut off the rough ends of the stems. Peel the stems and trim around the perimeter of the artichokes to remove any fibrous, tough dark green areas. Cut off the tips of the remaining tender leaves, then cut the artichokes lengthwise in half. Remove the choke, if you prefer.

3 • In a medium skillet, heat 1½ tablespoons of the butter over medium heat until melted. Add the artichokes and lemon juice and sauté for 2 or 3 minutes, until lightly browned. Add a scant ½ cup (100 ml) water, then cover and cook for 10 minutes, until tender. Set aside off the heat.

4 • Season the lamb with salt and pepper.

5 • In a large skillet, heat the remaining 2 tablespoons butter over high heat until melted. Add a drizzle of oil. Sear the rack of lamb in the pan for 5 minutes, turning to brown on all sides, then transfer the lamb to a baking dish. Bake for 5 minutes, or until you reach your desired doneness, 125 to 135°F (52 to 57°C) for medium rare. Allow to rest for 5 minutes and then slice between the ribs.

6 • Serve with the black olives and artichoke poivrade.

MON ASSIETTE ANGLAISE

(ROSBIF, SALADE, MAYONNAISE)

(Roast Beef, Green Salad, Mayonnaise)

Serves 2 to 4

Preparation time: 5 minutes
Cooking time: 20 minutes
Resting time: 2½ hours

---

boneless beef roast (such as a top loin roast or eye of round roast, about 1 pound 2 ounces/500 g)
2½ tablespoons unsalted butter
Salt and freshly ground black pepper
[illegible]/3 cup (150 g) Mayonnaise *(page 211)*
Salad greens dressed with Vinaigrette *(page 210)*, **for serving**

1 • Preheat the oven to 350°F (180°C).

2 • Place the beef roast in a baking dish and bring the meat to room temperature, around 30 minutes. Thinly slice the butter and distribute the slices on top of the roast. Season with salt and pepper.

3 • Bake for 20 minutes, or until the desired temperature is reached, 125°F (51°C for medium rare), when an instant-read thermometer is inserted in the center. Set the roast aside at room temperature for 1 hour, then refrigerate for 1 hour before slicing. Serve cold.

4 • Serve the roast beef slices with mayonnaise and the green salad.

FILET DE BOEUF SAUCE AU POIVRE SARAWAK

(Beef Filet Sarawak Peppercorn Sauce)

Serves 2

Preparation time: 5 minutes
Cooking time: 10 minutes

5 tablespoons (40 g) cracked black peppercorns (preferably Sarawak)
2 filet mignon steaks (about 7 ounces/200 g each), at room temperature (we use Normandie beef; substitute with your preferred high-quality local beef)
2 teaspoons unsalted butter
Salt
3 tablespoons Armagnac
Scant ½ cup (100 ml) crème fraîche
Scant ½ cup (100 ml) heavy cream (optional, but recommended)

1 • Place a skillet over high heat. Place the peppercorns in a shallow dish and roll the beef filets in them, pressing to ensure the meat is well crusted in the peppercorns.

2 • Place the filets in the hot pan and add the butter. Season with salt.

3 • Cook for 2 minutes on each side for a very rare steak, or cook them a little longer to the preferred level of doneness. Remove the filets and transfer them to a plate to rest for several minutes while preparing the sauce.

4 • Deglaze the pan with the Armagnac. Light the Armagnac with a long match and reduce the heat to low. Stir in the crème fraîche and a little of the heavy cream, if using. Cook for 5 minutes, or until the sauce thickens to a coating consistency. If the sauce looks separated, add a little more of the heavy cream as needed until the sauce becomes smooth again when stirred, or add more heavy cream to taste.

5 • Arrange the filets on 2 serving plates and top with the peppercorn sauce.

Tip: We always serve this with Fries (page 199)! This dish has become emblematic of Le Bistrot Paul Bert. We serve thousands every year.

PAUL BERT

PAUL BERT

ÉPAULE D'AGNEAU EN COCOTTE
ET HARICOTS TARBAIS

(Lamb Shoulder with Tarbais Beans)

erves 2

'eparation time: 5 minutes
ɔoking time: 25 minutes (lamb shoulder) plus 1 hour (beans)
esting time: Overnight

0½ ounces (300 g) dried Tarbais beans (or another white bean)
bouquet garni (see Tip, page 38)
yellow onion
½ tablespoons (50 g) unsalted butter
eutral-flavor oil
lamb shoulder (about 1 pound 5 ounces/600 g)
cant ½ cup (100 ml) dry white wine
alt and freshly ground black pepper
cant ½ cup (100 ml) water
hopped fresh herbs

1 • The day before, add the beans to a bowl of cold water to rehydrate them.

2 • The next day, preheat the oven to 350°F (180°C).

3 • Drain the beans and add them to a pot of water. Add 1 bouquet garni and cook over medium heat for 1 hour, or until tender. Drain.

4 • Peel and thinly slice the onion. In a Dutch oven over high heat, melt the butter with a drizzle of oil. Add the lamb shoulder and brown it on each side. Add the onion and cook for about 3 minutes, until softened. Deglaze the pot with the wine. Season with salt and pepper. Add the water and 1 bouquet garni. Bake for 25 to 45 minutes, covered, until it reaches your preferred level of doneness.

5 • Just before serving, remove the lamb shoulder from the Dutch oven. Transfer the beans to the lamb cooking juices, stir to combine, and then set the lamb shoulder on top of the beans. Garnish with herbs and then serve in the Dutch oven.

THE CHEF

1997 . . . 2000 . . . 2024

The years passed by, and so did the chefs. First, there was Sébastien, followed by John Euwer, a workaholic who would do anything to attract customers. He was passionate about cinema and theater, and his brother was an actor. His very classic cuisine delighted us for many months. Subsequent chefs brought a mix of personalities. Some were talented but temperamental. Others drank too much and were not very friendly, while others were friendly but not very good. One chef aspired to work at the Weston, another deliberately cut himself so he could leave in the middle of service, and a talented young chef de partie, who arrived dressed as a boy, left wearing a skirt and pigtails and blew me a kiss goodbye at the checkout. These were certainly not dull times! It wasn't always good, but there was plenty of laughter. Then, in June 2000, Thierry walked through the door. He was a young cook from Burgundy, diligent, hardworking, and seemingly ready to put up with me; little did he know what he was getting into when he accepted the job. We have experienced twenty-five years of hard work, spats, and arguments together. Thierry submitted his resignation twenty times, and I pretended to accept it twenty times! We make the perfect duo. He is focused on the work while I immerse myself in the theatrics; he wants to perform, and I want to direct.

Alone in front of his stove, Thierry interprets and coordinates a three-part score of sounds and aromas. His music is composed of butter sizzling and foaming in the pan, the noisy cascade of fries being plunged into the fryer, and the bubbling of the sauce *au poivre* as it gently reduces, its surface swelling and releasing small bursts of sonorous steam. The stove is cluttered, and the pots and pans clatter together. A waltz of voices and sounds continues nonstop, "stepping onto the stage" through the kitchen passthrough. Smoking pans are filled with food, and plates line the shelf in front of the stove. The heat and rich aromas that waft up when you lift a lid create the magic that is bistro cuisine of which Thierry is the master conductor.

Outside of the kitchen, the servers' voices chatter:

"Chef, for number 8, two settings, an *oeuf mayonnaise*, panfried porcini mushrooms, followed by a medium steak *au poivre*, a turbot with spring vegetables. Pay attention to the temperature of the filet, they are Americans . . ."

"Let me see the ticket. It's always the same! Medium-rare, well done! They know nothing . . ."

The washing machine gurgles as it fills up. Our dishwasher Niakasso has stood over a sink piled with dishes for fifteen years, banging them against each other! "Niakasso! Stop, it's Bernardaud china. It's worth tons. Be careful with the appetizers, no fingerprints on the plates. F . . . ! I keep repeating the same thing! They don't care! S . . . my filet!" Thierry applies pressure to a piece of meat using his gloved finger, gauging its doneness by the level of firmness he feels and the heat that rises to his fingertip.

Together, day after day, we have built a menu of appetizers, main courses, and desserts, all from the classics of bourgeois cuisine, integrating the fundamental principles of what was becoming known as bistronomy, namely a simple cuisine that gives pride of place to beautiful products from local terroir while respecting the seasons. Thierry is a true cook who works with his hands, an artisan in the noblest sense. He loves the taste of cream, butter, hearty stews, homemade sauces, reduced jus, and whole milk. His cuisine mirrors his character: sincere, sometimes brusque, and always consistent.

In his kitchen, there is no magic powder, no emulsifier, no gelling agents, no seafoam on a background of undergrowth, and no fuss over an *oeuf parfait*, which I might love or hate because it always seems imperfect to me.

Our hair has turned white over these twenty-five years, and we are like two crocodiles living together in the marshes. We maintain our space. With just a glance, we can gauge each other's moods. We don't always agree, as we each have our own quirks. I have preconceived notions about cooking, but I'm not a cook. He prefers to go fast, while I encourage him to take his time—of course, he retorts that he doesn't have the time!

mychef

THE VISIBILITY THEY DESERVE

Children's laughter can sometimes be heard in the restaurant's kitchen, mixed with discussions about soccer. My unexpected arrival often causes the chatter to abruptly stop. Naturally, no child plays soccer in the kitchen during dinner service, so where do these sounds come from? They originate from Mali, specifically the district of Kayes and the more remote village of Bandiougoula. Thanks to modern technology, our Malian employees can connect with their families and witness their children's lives in real time, even though their loved ones remain in their home villages. When families can't physically reunite, this faint connection allows our expatriate employees, who often stay away from home for several years, to continue fulfilling their roles as heads of households.

Over the past thirty years, we have experienced continuous waves of migration in the restaurant industry. Workers from Tunisia, Morocco, Sri Lanka, Bangladesh, and Mali have successively taken on some of the most challenging positions in our field, such as dishwashing or overnight cleaning crews. This influx of workers has gradually filled all the vacancies in our kitchens. These increasingly qualified laborers have become the backbone of our business. They are essential for our establishments, particularly in the kitchens. Many of our kitchen staff, from our dishwasher Niakasso to our sous chef Malé, are uncles, brothers, and cousins from the same villages. Some have been with us for three, ten, or even fifteen years, while others have left to pursue personal adventures.

Malé Traoré joined the bistro fifteen years ago and has since risen to become our second chef, working closely with our head chef, Thierry. In addition to his culinary duties, Malé manages an association for over two thousand Malian expatriates in France from his village. In this role, he acts as a community leader, bridging the gap between their culture and ours. When one side of the Mediterranean thrives, so does the other.

Everyone at the bistro works tirelessly, supporting one another and always willing to lend a helping hand. Like any family, we face misunderstandings, conflicts, and complications, particularly pertaining to religious viewpoints. We admittedly often encounter culture shock.

Our approach is to listen to our crew members and to assist them with their government paperwork. But don't get me wrong—we're not trying to be good Samaritans; we reject outdated paternalism. Instead, we aim to acknowledge their value to our crew and ensure they receive the recognition and respect they deserve in our society.

DOS DE CABILLAUD BEURRE BLANC

ET PETITS LÉGUMES

(Center-Cut Cod Fillets, Beurre Blanc, and Vegetables)

Serves 2

Preparation time: 10 minutes
Cooking time: 14 minutes

3½ ounces (100 g) broccoli florets
3½ ounces (100 g) cauliflower florets
1 carrot
Neutral-flavor oil
2 pieces center-cut cod fillets (about 5¼ ounces/150 g each)
Just over ¾ cup (200 ml) Beurre Blanc *(page 214)*
Salt and freshly ground black pepper

1 • Rinse the broccoli and cauliflower florets under cold running water. Peel the carrot, then cut it into rounds. Bring a pot of water to a boil and add the broccoli, cauliflower, and carrots. Cook for 4 minutes over high heat, until tender. Drain and set aside.

2 • Cut a piece of parchment paper the same diameter as the bottom of a medium skillet and place it in the bottom of the pan. Add a generous drizzle of oil, then add the fillets and cook over low heat until opaque, about 10 minutes.

3 • Add a little beurre blanc on 2 serving plates. Arrange the fish on top of the sauce and add the vegetables on the side. Season with salt and pepper. Serve.

Paul

LE BISTROT
PAUL BERT
Paris
LE BISTROT
PAUL BERT

SAUCISSE DU PERCHE ET PURÉE

(Sausage from Le Perche and Pureed Potatoes)

Serves 2

Preparation time: 5 minutes
Cooking time: 10 minutes

---

large (14-ounce/400-g) pork sausage (we source ours from Le Perche, a region in Normandy)
recipe Pureed Potatoes *(page 204)*
Salt and freshly ground black pepper
Chopped fresh herbs

1 • Preheat the oven to 400°F (200°C).

2 • In a medium skillet, panfry the sausage over high heat for 5 minutes on each side, until browned, then transfer it to a baking dish and bake for 5 minutes, until cooked through.

3 • Cut the sausage in half. Spoon the pureed potatoes on 2 serving plates and place a piece sausage on top. Season with salt and pepper and garnish with chopped herbs.

BOUDIN AUX POMMES

DE CHRISTIAN PARRA

(Christian Parra's Boudin Noir with Cooked Apples)

Serves 2

Preparation time: 5 minutes
Cooking time: 11 minutes

---

14 ounces (400 g) boudin noir (in the restaurant, we use the ones created by chef Christian Parra)
2 cooking apples
3½ tablespoons (50 g) unsalted butter
Chopped fresh herbs

1 • Cut the boudin into 2 thick slices, if not already cut.

2 • Peel the apples. Cut them in half and remove their cores. Cut the apples in half again.

3 • Cut a piece of parchment paper the same diameter as the bottom of a medium skillet and place it in the bottom of the pan. Add 1½ tablespoons of the butter to the pan. Melt the butter over high heat, then add the boudin slices arranged in stainless-steel cooking rings (the rings prevent them from breaking apart while cooking). Cook over low heat for 3 minutes on each side, until starting to crisp on both sides and warm all the way through. Remove the cooking rings and set the boudin slices aside and cover to keep warm.

4 • In a clean skillet over high heat, melt the remaining 2 tablespoons butter. Add the apple quarters and cook them over low heat for 5 minutes while swirling the pan to ensure even cooking. Serve the slices of boudin with the apples, garnished with fresh herbs.

Tip: In the restaurant, we also usually add a side of Pureed Potatoes (page 204).

BISTROT
PAUL BERT

PAUL BERT

PETIT SALÉ AUX LENTILLES

(Lentils with Salt Pork)

erves 2–4

reparation time: 10 minutes
ooking time: 2 hours 40 minutes

---

carrots
yellow onion
cloves
4 ounces (400 g) salt pork (pork chine and pork shoulder)
cups (400 g) Puy lentils
bouquet garni (see Tip, page 38)
alt and freshly ground black pepper
smoked pork sausages (we use Montbéliard sausages)
hopped fresh herbs and sliced red onion

1 • Peel the carrots and onion. Make 3 small incisions in the onion and press the cloves into them. Cut the carrots into rounds.

2 • Rinse the pork with water to remove excess salt. Bring a large pot of water to a boil and add the pork. Cook, covered, over low heat for 2 hours, until the pork is tender. Chop the pork into large pieces. Reserve the cooking liquid.

3 • Place the lentils, carrots, onion, and bouquet garni in a Dutch oven. Add just enough water to cover them. Season with salt and pepper. Bring to a boil and cook for about 20 minutes over medium-high heat. Add the cooked, chopped pieces of meat and sausages to the pot. If needed, add just over ¾ cup (200 ml) of the meat cooking juices to the pot to replace any evaporated liquid. Cook, uncovered, for an additional 20 minutes over medium heat, until the lentils are tender, the sausages are cooked through, and the liquid has been absorbed.

4 • Garnish with the sliced onions and chopped herbs and serve.

PICCATA DE VEAU

ET SES CONCHIGLIONI

(Veal Piccata with Conchiglioni)

Serves 2

Preparation time: 10 minutes
Cooking time: 14 minutes

4 white button mushrooms
1 sprig chervil (see Tip, page 65)
½ preserved lemon
10½ ounces (300 g) veal cushion
Salt
1½ tablespoons unsalted butter
Neutral-flavor oil
Scant ½ cup (100 g) crushed tomatoes
1 teaspoon crème fraîche
Freshly ground black pepper
7 ounces (200 g) conchiglioni pasta shells

1 • Briefly rinse the mushrooms under cold runnin water and cut off the rough ends from their stems. Rinse the chervil under a slow stream of cold wate Thoroughly dry them. Slice the mushrooms and chop the chervil. Chop the lemon. Thinly slice the veal cushion. Bring a medium pot of salted water to a boil.

2 • In a skillet, melt the butter over medium heat. Add a drizzle of oil. Fry the veal slices for several minutes on each side until lightly browned. Add the tomatoes, crème fraîche, and mushrooms to the pan and cook stirring occasionally for several minutes, until the mushrooms are softened and a creamy sauce forms. Season with salt and pepper. Add the chopped lemon and stir to combine. Set aside off the heat.

3 • Meanwhile, add the conchiglioni to the pot of boiling water. Cook for about 9 minutes, until al dente. Drain and set aside.

4 • On 2 serving plates, neatly arrange the veal slices and place the conchiglioni on the side. Ladle some of the sauce from the pan around the slices and drizzle on the pasta. Sprinkle with the chopped chervil.

LE BISTROT
PAUL BERT

DOS DE LIEU JAUNE RÔTI

ET ENDIVES BRAISÉES AU JUS DE VIANDE

(Center-Cut Roasted Fish Steaks with Braised Belgian Endives)

Serves 2

Preparation time: 10 minutes
Cooking time: 30 minutes

---

4 medium Belgian endives
3½ tablespoons (50 g) unsalted butter
Just over ¾ cup (200 ml) Veal Stock *(page 217)*
Neutral-flavor oil
2 fish steaks, skin on, center-cut (about 7 ounces/200 g each) (preferably pollock, if not cod or haddock)
Salt and freshly ground black pepper

1 • Rinse the endives under cold running water and thoroughly pat them dry using paper towels. Cut off the rough ends. In a large skillet over high heat, heat 1½ tablespoons of the butter. When the butter is melted, add the endives and reduce the heat to medium. Braise for 10 minutes on each side while basting them regularly with the melted butter in the pan. When the endives are well caramelized, deglaze the pan with a little of the veal stock and cook for an additional 2 minutes, constantly basting them with the cooking juices. Set aside off the heat.

2 • Cut a piece of parchment paper the same diameter as the bottom of a medium skillet and place it in the bottom of the pan. You can use the same pan used for cooking the endives, but clean it first. Add a generous drizzle of oil to the pan over high heat. Add the remaining 2 tablespoons butter. When the butter has completely melted and is foaming slightly, add the fish steaks skin side down and reduce the heat to low. Cook until the steaks are opaque, about 10 minutes.

3 • Arrange the fish steaks on 2 serving plates skin side down. Add the braised endives around the fish. Spoon some of the cooking juices over the top, season with salt and pepper, and serve.

SAUMON BROCOLI

ET MAYONNAISE À L'AIL DES OURS

(Salmon, Broccoli, and Wild Garlic Mayonnaise)

rves 2

eparation time: 10 minutes
ooking time: 11 minutes

½ ounces (300 g) broccoli
bouquet garni (see Tip, page 38)
salmon fillets (about 5¼ ounces/150 g) each
alt and freshly ground black pepper
cup (150 g) Mayonnaise *(page 211)*, **flavored with wild garlic**

1 • Rinse the broccoli under cold running water and cut it into florets.

2 • Bring a large pot of water to a boil and add the florets and the bouquet garni. Cook over medium heat for 6 minutes, until bright green and crisp tender. Immediately transfer them to a bowl of ice water to stop the cooking and maintain their color. After about 1 minute, drain, and set aside.

3 • Bring a separate saucepan of water to a boil. Place the salmon fillets in a steamer basket and place the basket on top of the pan of boiling water. Cook over medium heat for 5 minutes, or until fish flakes easily and has reached your desired doneness.

4 • Serve each salmon fillet seasoned with salt and pepper, accompanied by the broccoli florets and a little wild garlic mayonnaise.

Tip: This dish is also delicious served cold!

CÔTE DE COCHON DU PERCHE

ET SES POMMES DE TERRE RÔTIES

(Pork from Le Perche and Roasted Potatoes)

Serves 2 to 4

Preparation time: 5 minutes
Cooking time: 30 minutes

---

14 ounces (400 g) baby potatoes (as small as possible)

7 tablespoons (100 g) unsalted butter

Neutral-flavor oil

1 pound 2 ounces (500 g) pork rib chops (we source ours from Le Perche)

Salt and freshly ground black pepper

4 cloves garlic, unpeeled

1 large shallot, unpeeled

Chopped fresh herbs

1 • Preheat the oven to 350°F (180°C).

2 • Rinse the potatoes under cold running water and pat them dry. Cut them in half if they are too big, otherwise leave them whole. Set aside.

3 • In a large skillet over high heat, heat 3½ tablespoons (50 g) of the butter. Add a drizzle of oil and place the pork in the pan. Season with salt and pepper and cook for about 5 minutes on each side, until browned.

4 • Transfer the pork to a baking dish with the potatoes, unpeeled garlic cloves, and unpeeled shallot. Cut the remaining 3½ tablespoons (50 g) butter into cubes and add it to the baking dish. Bake for 15 minutes, until the meat reaches 145°F (63°C) when measured with an instant-read thermometer. Allow to rest for 5 minutes and then slice. The pork should be cooked to a rosy-pink color.

5 • Sprinkle with fresh herbs and serve.

SUPRÊME DE VOLAILLE SAUCE SAVAGNIN

ET MORILLES

(Chicken Breast Savagnin Wine and Morel Sauce)

erves 2

'eparation time: 10 minutes
esting time: 1 hour
ooking time: 40 minutes

---

ounce (25 g) dried morel mushrooms
½ tablespoons (50 g) unsalted butter
boneless, skinless chicken breasts
cant ½ cup (100 ml) Savagnin wine (or vin jaune)
cant ½ cup (100 ml) heavy cream
hopped fresh herbs

1 • Rehydrate the morels by immersing them in a bowl of cool water for 1 hour. Gently clean the morels under a slow stream of cold water and thoroughly pat them dry using a clean towel or paper towels.

2 • In a small skillet over high heat, heat 1½ tablespoons of the butter. Add the morels and sauté for 5 minutes while stirring constantly, until softened and buttery. Set aside off the heat.

3 • In a clean large skillet over high heat, melt the remaining 2 tablespoons butter. Add the chicken breasts. Reduce the heat and cook, covered, for 15 minutes. Increase the heat and cook, uncovered, for 3 to 4 minutes to brown them. Deglaze the pan with the wine.

4 • Set the chicken breasts aside on a plate and tent to keep warm. Add the cream and morels to the pan and cook over medium heat for 15 minutes, until the flavors are well combined and the sauce has thickened.

5 • Serve the chicken breasts topped with the morel sauce and garnished with herbs.

Tip: We prefer to use fresh morels in the restaurant, but they require longer cooking times and expertise to handle correctly. Fresh, raw morels are toxic so are not recommended for home use.

LE BISTROT
PAUL BERT
Paris
LE BISTROT
PAUL BERT

PERNOD 51

LAPIN À LA MOUTARDE

(Rabbit in Mustard Sauce)

Serves 2

Preparation time: 10 minutes
Cooking time: 1 hour 5 minutes

---

1 yellow onion
1 clove garlic
1½ tablespoons unsalted butter
2 full rabbit legs
Scant ½ cup (100 ml) dry white wine
⅔ cup (150 g) crème fraîche
1 bouquet garni (see Tip, page 38)
Salt and freshly ground black pepper
1 bunch tarragon
1 tablespoon Dijon mustard

1 • Peel and thinly slice the onion. Peel and halve the garlic clove. Remove and discard any sprouts from the center of the clove. Crush the garlic using the flat side of a knife blade.

2 • Heat the butter in a Dutch oven over medium heat and add the rabbit. Cook for several minutes, until browned on both sides. Add the sliced onion and crushed garlic. Cook for several seconds, then deglaze the pan with the wine. Add the crème fraîche and bouquet garni. Using a wooden spoon, stir to thoroughly combine. Season with salt and pepper. Reduce the heat to low and cook, covered, for 1 hour, until the rabbit meat is tender and the leg joint bends easily.

3 • Rinse the tarragon under a slow stream of cold water. Thoroughly pat it dry using paper towels, then chop it. Remove the legs from the pot. Add the mustard and blend the cooking liquid using an immersion blender until smooth. Add the tarragon and then serve.

LE BISTROT
PAUL BERT
RÉSERVATIONS
UNIQUEMENT
Paris
PAR TELÉPHONE
01 43 72 24 01
18 RUE PAUL BERT, 75011

THE VEGETABLE GARDEN
IN LES ESSARTS

The van has just pulled up in front of the bistro. Greg, our vegetable gardener, is unloading his boxes of vegetables. The crates are lined up on the sidewalk, containing peas, haricots verts, the season's first fennel, cilantro, chervil, and new potatoes. Passersby stop to look at and admire the abundant display. As the season progresses, the boxes' contents will change.

About ten years ago, we came up with the idea for a vegetable garden at a time when restaurant owners were starting to take an interest in vegetables, their provenance, and how they are grown. It is important to give credit where credit is due: The mad cow disease crisis in 2001 and the influence of the renowned three-star chef Alain Passard played a crucial role in moving vegetables to the center of the plate. Before this time, vegetables were often seen as a mere accompaniment, overshadowed by high-protein dishes. Chef Passard boldly decided to focus on vegetables, stepping away from meat—though he would later return to it—and began cultivating haute couture vegetables by setting up his first vegetable garden in Normandy.

Returning to the topic of our garden: At the time, the property we owned in Le Perche had never been cultivated and was a pristine environment, so the decision to create the Potager des Essarts was an obvious one. I was well aware that we could not produce all the vegetables we needed year-round, so the vegetable garden needed to focus on local varieties. The goal was to promote high-quality, chemical-free produce that would transform our customers' perceptions and tastes regarding vegetables.

Our first order of business was to plant fruit trees, including apples, plums, and cherries. We surrounded the plot with hazelnut hedges and established intermediate rows of currants, raspberries, and blackcurrants. This setup would help protect the future beds of peas, haricots verts, yellow beans, fennel, and aromatic plants. Additionally, we included zucchini, cornichons, new potatoes, Jerusalem artichokes, beets, and other root vegetables.

We slowly put everything in place. We added three open-ground greenhouses, unheated, allowing us to produce about twenty varieties of tomatoes from July to October, much to the delight of our Parisian customers.

Three beehives and a few chickens were eventually invited to contribute to the ecosystem: the bees for pollination, the chickens for biodiversity and to help control certain pests such as slugs and other salad-damaging insects. Retired mules and horses were brought in to assist in maintaining the fields while adding charm to the landscape.

Some plots surrounding the vegetable garden are left fallow or mowed very late in the year to preserve the existing ecosystem. This practice supports the reproduction of wild species, such as hares and gray partridges, as well as the millions of crawling and flying insects that enrich our living heritage. This approach, while somewhat minimalist and not necessarily profitable, has three strengths and one aspiration, in my view:

- The production of healthy and tasty vegetables. Nothing makes me happier than hearing customers rave about rediscovering the flavor of tomatoes or haricots verts they haven't enjoyed since childhood.
- Respect for the environment by giving back to nature and society a portion of what we take to support our business.
- The creation of sustainable employment in a particularly difficult region and sector.
- Aspiring to organize the recycling of food waste from our restaurants to produce high-quality compost.

This emotional connection to the pastoral world, which I have aimed to incorporate into this project, is not merely a passing Parisian trend. It also enables me to communicate to our customers that we are dedicated participants in the ecology of the future. We strive to produce healthy fruits and vegetables at fair prices sourced directly from local suppliers to our restaurants without the involvement of third parties.

Gilac

RECIPES FROM OUR SEAFOOD-FOCUSED RESTAURANT NEXT DOOR TO LE BISTROT PAUL BERT

LLER
STROT

BRETAGNE
Plates du Belon
Speciales
Fines
PLATEAU
Praires
Clams
Palourdes
Amandes

NORMANDIE
Speciales Utah beach
Pleine mer
DE MER
Etrilles
Oursins
Tourteaux
Crevettes
Araignées
Bouquet breton
CADORET
CADORET

OYSTERS,
A FAMILY TRADITION

by Gwénaëlle Cadoret

From the very beginning of the adventure of what became Bistrot Paul Bert, alongside Bertrand, we aimed to showcase my family's cultural heritage by opening, just next door, a seafood-focused establishment, L'Écailler du Bistrot.

For five generations, my family has been passionately dedicated to raising oysters in Brittany on nearly five hundred acres (two hundred hectares) of parks between the Belon River and the Bay of Carantec.

At L'Écailler du Bistrot, we proudly feature the oysters we cultivate.

There are three kinds of oysters: "*fines*," "*spéciales*," which are in fact cupped oysters from a Japanese strain imported in the 1970s, and Belon oysters, also called European flats, whose origin is local.

The difference between *fines* and *spéciales* is primarily found in the farming method, the number of shellfish per square meter, and the location of the oyster beds.

The *fines* are cultivated in the open sea. They are brinier, more saline, and not very fleshy. They are commonly referred to as *creuses* de Bretagne.

The *spéciales*, raised in rivers where the sea water mixes with fresh water, are more fleshy, crunchy, and tender.

In contrast, Belons are known for their round, flat shape and are very delicate. Although they lost their AOP (Protected Designation of Origin) status, they are still regarded as the queen of oysters, especially when we cultivate them in their native beds along the Belon River. Belons are characterized by a long mouthfeel, a subtle bitterness, and a distinctive nutty flavor.

The quality of oysters can vary significantly depending on the region and the expertise of the oyster farmer. As skilled artisans of the sea, oyster farmers understand which beds yield specific characteristics. They may move their oysters from one bed to another for refinement to achieve their desired results. This process, a true craft that mixes tradition with family heritage, is akin to the work of a winemaker who navigates the cultivation of vines, explores a variety of grape types, and blends different juices.

To enjoy these delicious shellfish to the fullest, follow these guidelines for optimal tasting:

- Never serve oysters over ice, as excessive cold can diminish their flavors.
- Discard the water found in the shell immediately after opening them.
- Take care not to damage the flesh while opening the oyster.

For the briny and salty *fines*, minimal seasoning is best. They can be paired with lemon, shallot vinegar, or even Japanese rice vinegar.

The *spéciales* should be seasoned lightly to preserve their complex flavor profile. However, a sprinkle of freshly ground Sarawak black pepper can enhance their taste.

The Belons, known for their strong character, pair well with a touch of lemon or Sarawak pepper.

LES HUITRES
CADORET

L'ECAILLER
DU BISTROT

HOMARD RÔTI AU KARI GOSSE

(Roasted Lobster in Kari Gosse Cream)

erves 2

reparation time: 10 minutes
ooking time: 25 minutes

⅔ cups (400 ml) heavy cream

teaspoons Kari Gosse (a proprietary spice mixture from Brittany made of ginger, chile, black pepper, cloves, cinnamon, and turmeric; order online, or substitute with your own spice blend)

alt

whole lobster with claws (about 1 pound 12 ounces/800 g)

1 • Preheat the oven to 350°F (180°C).

2 • In a small saucepan, heat the cream and Kari Gosse over medium heat. Season with salt. Cook, stirring regularly, to reduce by half, about 10 minutes, until the mixture is very smooth. Watch it very closely!

3 • Cut the lobster lengthwise in half. Snap off the claws. Spoon 1 tablespoon of sauce over each lobster half. Place under the broiler for about 15 minutes, until the meat is opaque and reaches 135 to 140°F (57 to 60°C) when measured with an instant-read thermometer.

4 • Spoon the remaining sauce over the lobster halves.

Tip: Serve with a side of Fries (page 199)!

SOLE MEUNIÈRE

(Panfried Sole)

Serves 2

Preparation time: 5 minutes
Cooking time: 8 to 10 minutes

1 whole sole (about 1 pound 2 ounces/500 g), prepared by your fishmonger, skin removed
2½ tablespoons all-purpose flour
3½ tablespoons (50 g) unsalted butter
Salt and freshly ground black pepper
1 recipe Boiled Potatoes *(page 206)*
Lemon wedges
Melted butter

1 • Dredge the sole in the flour, gently shake off any excess, and set aside.

2 • In a large skillet, cook the butter over medium heat until melted and lightly browned. Add the sole to the pan and cook for 4 to 5 minutes on each side, until browned. Remove the skin and season with salt and pepper before serving. Serve with the boiled potatoes, lemon, and melted butter (see Tip).

Tip: This recipe can be served two ways: Either generously top the fish with melted butter and a dash of lemon juice or serve it dry with the melted butter and lemon in a gravy boat on the side.

L'ECAILLE

L'ECAILLER
DU BISTROT

CARPACCIO DE BAR

(Sea Bass Carpaccio)

erves 2

reparation time: 10 minutes

½ lemon
0½ ounces (300 g) line-caught sea bass
cant ½ cup (100 ml) cold-pressed extra-virgin olive oil
¾ ounce (20 g) bottarga di tonno (salted cured fish roe), very dry

1 • Juice the lemon and set aside.

2 • Very thinly slice the bass. Neatly arrange the slices on 2 serving plates.

3 • Add the oil and lemon juice to a bowl and whisk vigorously to combine.

4 • Just before serving, pour a little of the lemon oil over the fish. Grate some bottarga over the top.

PÂTES AUX OURSINS

(*Sea Urchin Pasta*)

Serves 2

Preparation time: 10 minutes
Cooking time: 10 minutes

---

2 large whole sea urchins
3 chives
2⅛ ounces (60 g) spaghetti noodles, preferably made with Khorasan (Kamut) flour (a low-gluten flour)
2 tablespoons crème fraîche
Salt and freshly ground pepper

1 • Carefully open the sea urchins using kitchen shears to cut out the beak and then continue cuttin to enlarge the opening so that you can access and remove the roe. Clean the roe using cold water and then place them on a piece of parchment paper and set aside. Cut the opening in the urchin shells to make it larger and smooth the edges, if necessary, to form a bowl-like shape that will be easy to fill with noodles.

2 • Clean out the sea urchin shells by rinsing then with cold water, then place them upside down on paper towels to drain.

3 • Rinse the chives under a slow stream of cold water. Thoroughly pat them dry.

4 • Bring a pot of water to a boil. Add the spaghett noodles and boil for 6 minutes, or just until al dente

5 • While the spaghetti is cooking, add a ladle of the cooking water to a large skillet over low heat. Drain the spaghetti and add it to the skillet. Add the crème fraîche, then half of the sea urchin roe and the chives. Season with salt and pepper. Let the sauce reduce for 3 to 4 minutes, about the time it takes for the noodles to finish cooking.

6 • Fill the sea urchin shells with the noodles. Just before serving, place the remaining roe on top.

L'ECAILLER
DU BISTROT

ÉMINCÉ DE POMMES GLACE VANILLE

CARAMEL SALÉ

(Sliced Apples, Vanilla Ice Cream, Salted Caramel)

erves 2

reparation time: 20 minutes
ooking time: 35 minutes

---

or the Crumble

cup (75 g) all-purpose flour
cup plus 2½ teaspoons (60 g) sugar
½ tablespoons (35 g) unsalted butter, cut into cubes and softened, plus more, melted, for brushing the apples

Pink Lady apples
cup (250 ml) vanilla ice cream

or the Salted Caramel Sauce

cup (50 g) sugar
cup (50 g) heavy cream
inch salt

• Preheat the oven to 350°F (180°C).

• Make the crumble: Add the flour and sugar into medium mixing bowl and stir to combine. Add the nsalted butter and combine using your hands to nake a sandy texture.

• Spread the crumble in an even layer on a aking sheet and bake for about 15 minutes, until olden.

4 • While the crumble is baking, prepare the apples. Grease a piece of parchment paper and set on a baking sheet. Peel, core, and quarter the apples, and then very thinly slice them (use a mandoline, if available). Overlap the slices to form 2 circular shapes, approximately 6 inches (15 cm) in diameter each, on the parchment paper. Carefully brush the apple slices with melted butter.

5 • Set the crumble aside to cool and bake the apples for 15 minutes, or until softened.

6 • While the apples are baking, make the salted caramel sauce: In a small heavy-bottom saucepan, melt the sugar until caramelized, gently swirling the pan a few times. Do not stir and watch it carefully to prevent it from burning. When the caramel is a medium amber color, 2 to 3 minutes, reduce the heat and add the cream. The mixture will bubble up, so be cautious. Add a pinch of salt and, using a wooden spoon, stir well to blend into a smooth, pourable sauce. Set aside over very low heat to keep warm.

7 • Using a wide spatula, carefully transfer the baked apple rosettes to serving plates. Add a scoop of vanilla ice cream in the center. Drizzle the caramel sauce over the top and spoon the crumble around the edges. Serve.

Tip: If you have leftover crumble, store it for up to a week in an airtight container away from humidity.

CREVETTES
ROSES BIO

Etrilles
BULOTS

L'ECAILLER

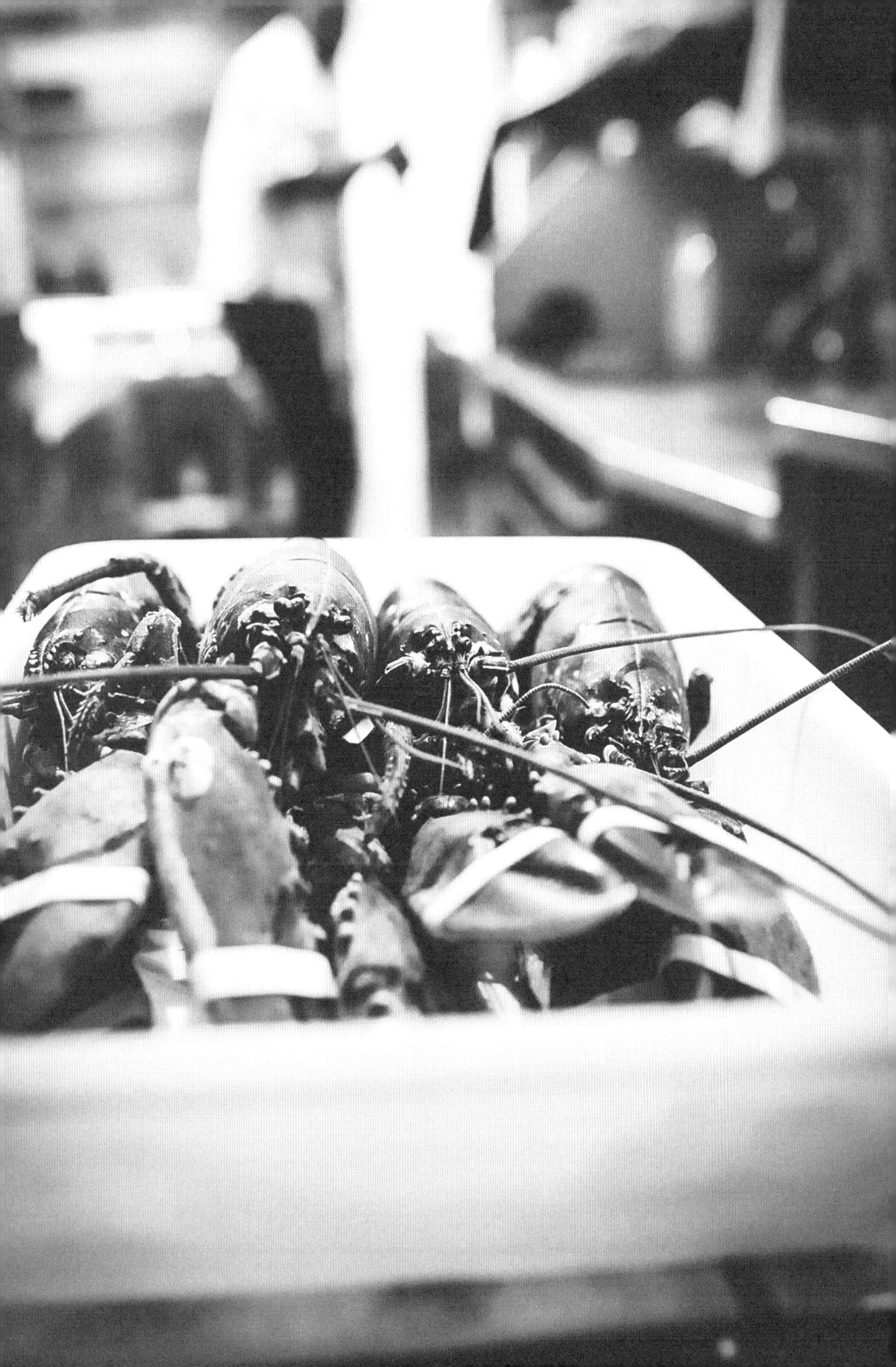

ACCOMP
& SA

NIMENTS

UCES

CUISSON DES LÉGUMES VERTS

(*Boiled Green Vegetables*)

Serves 2

Preparation time: 5 minutes
Cooking time: 3 to 5 minutes
Resting time: 10 minutes

10½ ounces (300 g) assorted green vegetables
Salt

1 • Rinse the vegetables under cold running water. Bring a pot of salted water to a boil, then add the vegetables. Cook over medium heat for 3 to 5 minutes. The cooking time will depend on the size of the vegetables. Haricots verts, for example, will cook in less time than broccoli.

2 • Test for doneness by inserting the tip of a knife into the vegetables while they are cooking. If they feel too firm, continue cooking for several more seconds.

3 • Immediately transfer the vegetables to a bowl of ice water to immediately stop the cooking. Set aside for 10 minutes, then drain.

FRITES

(Fries)

erves 2

·eparation time: 15 minutes
esting time: 2 hours
·eparation time: about 10 minutes

---

eanut oil, for deep frying
pound 2 ounces (500 g) russet potatoes
alt

1 • Preheat a deep fryer or large heavy pot with oil to 320°F (160°C).

2 • Peel the potatoes, then cut them into ⅓-inch-thick (1 cm) sticks. (The length of each one should be the equivalent to the length of the potato.)

3 • Fry them in the hot oil for 5 minutes to parcook (they should remain pale in color). Transfer the fries to a rack set on a rimmed baking sheet to drain. Set aside for 2 hours.

4 • Preheat the deep fryer or large heavy pot with oil to 350°F (180°C). Fry the potatoes again, to the desired level of crispness (about 5 minutes if you like them golden).

5 • Drain the fries, season with salt, and serve immediately.

WINES, VINES, AND WINEGROWERS

This morning, a crisis unit had gathered in my office. Everyone present seemed to be against me: my beloved wife, my bookkeeper, and my CPA, who, although shaking his head at me, was also laughing under his breath. The matter seemed rather grave. The time had come to own up, and I was the one being rebuked.

The issue? The bistro's wine inventory had increased by another fifteen percent in volume. The number of bottles had reached an astronomical number for a modest neighborhood bistro: thirty thousand, amounting to several hundred thousand euros in value, with five hundred labels offered on the menu and more than eight hundred different labels in all.

To reach this point, I had simply stuck to the advice of my mentor, Michel Picard. One day, he took me aside to whisper to me: "Don't bother so much with the food. Keep it simple and focus on a large wine list at reasonable prices. It's better to have wine in the cellar than cash in the bank. If everything goes wrong, at least we will always have something to drink."

A bistro simply cannot exist without wine, encompassing a wide array of reds, whites, rosés, and even orange wines (a skin-fermented white wine), spanning from extravagant Grands Crus to classic oaky Bordeaux to natural wines, which are often as praised as they are detested.

Our selection is rich in exceptional and unique bottles resulting from the daily efforts of thousands of winegrowers. Each winemaker has a story to tell and implements a philosophy centered around respect for their terroir as well as a careful approach to their work with the vines and in the cellars. This richness and diversity creates a fascinating mosaic of passionate individuals with a wide range of personalities and backgrounds: rural winegrowers; social activists who grew up during the protests of 1968 and who eventually settled deep in the Ardèche; a visionary former beekeeper from Tavel; distinguished families from Burgundy; a dreamer who restored the reputation of Jura wines; a family that transformed the history of wine in Corsica, from father to son; and a domaine in Côtes du Rhône known for its legendary Mémé cuvée, which fundamentally changed my taste and approach to wine. Additionally, some have brought recognition to Gamay, the sensational grape variety from Beaujolais, from Fleurie to Côte du Py to Saint-Amour. Certainly, Beaujolais offers more than just what is "nouveau."

Let's take a moment, even if it is not generally where I prefer to focus, to reflect on the moguls, insurers, and bankers who play a game somewhat like Monopoly in Bordeaux and beyond. They have quickly recognized that French luxury products—encompassing everything from champagne to grand Bordeaux and Burgundies—generate profits that rival, or even exceed, those of high-end perfumes and Hermès handbags.

We cannot deny that this vision of luxury, paired with exceptional gastronomy, enables France's wines to shine across the globe, and these remarkable wines are what draw foreign customers to our bistros.

Not long after we opened, my decision was made. More than twenty years ago, we opted to make room in our cellars for natural wines, while maintaining a selection of the grand classics and winemakers with diverse approaches. Even though I was not a wine fanatic at the time and lacked specific technical knowledge, I always championed the values of taste and pleasure, recognizing that these aspects are not the same to everyone. Although our approach may seem obvious now, it was less evident in the early 2000s. Our wine list has primarily been built on the winemakers whose principles respect terroir, eliminate the use of pesticides in vineyards, practice sustainable farming, avoid additives in the winemaking process, use indigenous yeast exclusively, and minimize, as much as possible, the quantity of added sulfites.

But we have also built our selection considering our customers' preferences, including those who may enjoy more mature, classic wines.

Returning to the core of this story, we have a vast selection of wines, and the financial implications are significant. However, we strive to maintain a vibrant inventory for the enjoyment of our customers and for the winemakers who appreciate that we aim to release their wines when they are at their best. This is also beneficial for professionals, restaurateurs, sommeliers, and oenologists who are always on the lookout for the perfect bottle, vintage, or unique winemaker they have yet to taste.

In conclusion, I admit it: "Mea culpa, mea culpa!" Yes, I buy too much wine. I am a perpetually dissatisfied collector, constantly searching for that undiscovered winemaker. Despite my efforts to change, I remain stuck in my ways, much like the scorpion in the fable of the scorpion and the frog, in which the scorpion asks the frog to help him cross the river, yet still stings him, knowing it will lead to his demise. It is just his nature.

PURÉE

(Pureed Potatoes)

Serves 2

Preparation time: 15 minutes
Cooking time: 20 minutes

2 tablespoons unsalted butter, softened
10½ ounces (300 g) yellow or Yukon Gold potatoes
Salt
3 tablespoons (150 ml) heavy cream
3 tablespoons (150 ml) whole milk
Pinch freshly grated nutmeg
Freshly ground black pepper

1 • Cut the butter into small cubes.

2 • Peel the potatoes. Add them to a bowl of cold water to prevent browning. Bring a medium pot of salted water to a boil. Add the potatoes and cook at a simmer over medium heat for 20 minutes, or until a knife pierces a potato easily.

3 • Thoroughly drain the potatoes, then process them through a food mill or potato ricer into a bowl.

4 • Add the butter and stir to melt it in, then add the cream, milk, and nutmeg. Mix the puree using a fork until the ingredients are incorporated. Season with salt and pepper.

POMMES DE TERRE FONDANTES

(Butter-Roasted "Melting" Potatoes)

erves 2

reparation time: 5 minutes
ooking time: 30 minutes

- **½ tablespoons (50 g) unsalted butter**
- **ounces (200 g) yellow or Yukon Gold potatoes**

1 • Preheat the oven to 350°F (180°C).

2 • In a small saucepan over high heat, heat the butter until melted and lightly browned. Set aside off the heat.

3 • Peel the potatoes and cut them in half.

4 • Brush a rimmed baking sheet with a little of the melted butter using a basting brush.

5 • Arrange the potato halves cut side down on the baking sheet. Brush them with the melted butter.

6 • Bake for 30 minutes, until the potatoes are tender inside and golden brown on the cut side.

POMMES DE TERRE À L'ANGLAISE

(Boiled Potatoes)

Serves 2

Preparation time: 5 minutes
Cooking time: 20 minutes

7 ounces (200 g) yellow or Yukon Gold potatoes
Salt

1 • Peel the potatoes.

2 • Bring a pot of salted water to a boil. As soon as the water is boiling, add the potatoes. Cook over medium heat until tender when pierced with a fork, about 20 minutes, then drain.

POMMES DE TERRE SAUTÉES

(Sautéed Potatoes)

erves 2

reparation time: 5 minutes
ooking time: 15 minutes

---

ounces (200 g) yellow or Yukon Gold potatoes
½ tablespoons (50 g) unsalted butter
eutral-flavor oil
alt and freshly ground black pepper

1 • Peel the potatoes and very thinly slice them, preferably using a mandoline.

2 • In a large skillet over medium heat, melt the butter with a light drizzle of oil. When the butter has completely melted, add the thin slices of potatoes, increase the heat to high, and cook for 15 minutes, stirring occasionally, or until the potatoes are a light golden brown on both sides.

3 • Season with salt and pepper.

VINAIGRETTE

Serves 2

Preparation time: 5 minutes

2 tablespoons Dijon mustard
1 tablespoon sherry vinegar
Salt and freshly ground black pepper
¼ cup (60 ml) olive oil
1 tablespoon peanut oil

1 • In a small bowl, combine the mustard and vinegar. Season with salt and pepper, then whisk until thoroughly incorporated.

2 • Add the oils in a very light drizzle while whisking as vigorously as possible. The incorporation of air into the preparation will give it a creamy, thickened consistency.

MAYONNAISE

erves 2

reparation time: 10 minutes

tablespoon Dijon mustard
uice of ½ lemon
large (20 g) egg yolk
alt and freshly ground black pepper
tablespoons (75 ml) peanut oil
plash of sherry vinegar

1 • In a small bowl, combine the mustard, lemon juice, and egg yolk. Season with salt and pepper, then whisk until thoroughly blended.

2 • Add the oil in a very light drizzle while whisking as vigorously as possible. Continue adding the oil in this way while whisking until the mixture is smooth and creamy.

3 • Add the vinegar and stir to thoroughly incorporate.

Tip: You can season your mayonnaise in endless ways, such as by adding chopped fresh herbs, finely grated garlic cloves, spices, or fish roe. If you want to make truffle mayonnaise, replace the peanut oil with truffle oil and stir in 1 teaspoon of chopped truffle shavings.

TARTAR SAUCE

Serves 2

Preparation time: 15 minutes

2 shallots
1 bunch tarragon
1 teaspoon capers
1 tablespoon Dijon mustard
1 large (20 g) egg yolk
Salt and freshly ground black pepper
5 tablespoons (75 ml) peanut oil
Splash of sherry vinegar

1 • Peel and finely chop the shallots.

2 • Rinse the tarragon under a slow stream of colc water. Thoroughly pat it dry, then chop it.

3 • Drain and finely chop the capers. Set aside.

4 • In a small bowl, whisk together the mustard and egg yolk. Season with salt and pepper, then whisk until thoroughly combined.

5 • Add the oil in a very light drizzle while whisking as vigorously as possible. Continue adding the oil i this way while whisking until the mixture is smooth and creamy.

6 • Add the vinegar, shallots, tarragon, and capers

7 • Whisk until smooth.

LE PAUL BERT
à la carte
Terrine de Campagne maison
LE PAUL BERT
à la carte
Terrine de Campagne maison

BEURRE BLANC

(*White Wine Butter Sauce*)

Serves 2

Preparation time: 5 minutes
Resting time: 30 minutes
Cooking time: 25 minutes

7 tablespoons (100 g) unsalted butter
2 shallots
½ teaspoon sherry vinegar
Just over ¾ cup (200 ml) dry white wine

1 • Remove the butter from the refrigerator 30 minutes before starting the recipe. Cut it into cubes.

2 • Peel and finely chop the shallots. Place the shallots in a small saucepan. Add the vinegar and white wine, then reduce over medium heat for about 20 minutes, until the liquid has almost completely evaporated.

3 • Add the butter cubes while emulsifying using a whisk. Continue whisking until the butter is fully incorporated and the mixture is creamy.

BEURRE CITRONNÉ

(Lemon Butter)

erves 2

reparation time: 2 minutes
ooking time: 10 minutes

½ tablespoons (50 g) unsalted butter
uice of ½ lemon

1 • Cut the butter into cubes and put it in a saucepan over medium heat. When the butter is completely melted, spoon out the clarified butter (the clearest liquid concentrated on the surface) and transfer it to a bowl.

2 • Add the lemon juice to the clarified butter and vigorously whisk to combine.

SAUCE AU VIN JAUNE

(Vin Jaune [Yellow Wine] Sauce)

Serves 2

Cooking time: 15 minutes

---

1 cup (250 ml) chicken stock
Scant ½ cup (100 ml) vin jaune or Savagnin wine
Scant ½ cup (100 ml) heavy cream
Salt and freshly ground black pepper

1 • In a small skillet over medium heat, simmer the chicken stock for about 10 minutes to reduce it. Add the vin jaune and reduce the liquid over medium heat for an additional 5 minutes, until a thin gravy forms.

2 • Stir in the cream. Taste and season with salt and pepper as needed.

FOND DE VEAU

(Veal Stock)

Makes about 2 cups (500 ml)
Preparation time: 5 minutes
Cooking time: 75 hours

---

1 carrot
1 yellow onion
1 stalk celery
3 or 4 medium veal bones (ideally with a tiny bit of flesh still attached)
Just over ¾ cup (200 ml) dry white wine
4 sprigs lemon thyme
2 bay leaves
1 calf's foot

1 • Preheat the oven to 350°F (180°C).

2 • Peel the carrot and onion and cut them in half. Cut the celery into sections. Set aside.

3 • Place the veal bones in a large Dutch oven. Bake, uncovered, just until they begin to brown, about 30 minutes. Remove any excess fat from the pot.

4 • Place the pot with the bones over medium heat. Cook for 2 to 3 minutes, then add the wine to deglaze the pot. Add the thyme, bay leaves, carrot, onion, and celery and cook until the vegetables have softened and the wine is absorbed, 2 to 3 minutes. Reduce heat to low.

5 • Add water to the pot 3 times the volume of the contents. Cut the calf's foot in half and add it to the pot. Cook covered for 72 hours over low heat, adding a little water from time to time to maintain the same volume of water.

6 • Strain, reserving the cooking liquid. Add the cooking liquid back to the pot and cook uncovered over low heat until reduced to a thick consistency, about 2½ hours.

THE PRODUCERS
AND THE SEASONS

Farmers, breeders, market gardeners, harvesters, winegrowers, fishermen, oyster farmers, bakers, mushroom foragers, and coffee merchants are the backbone of our profession. Their dedication and hard work, which follow the rhythm of the seasons, enhance our menus and daily specials. We have a close relationship with all of them, and they keep us informed about their progress and alert us to any potential weather hazards. The morning I wrote this, Gildas, my fish buyer from Guilvinec, called to warn me, "There's a storm over here. It's blowing hard, no one went out last night. We won't have many fish at the auction. Prices will be on the rise." He sensed a little disappointment and said to me, nervously: "OK, don't make a fuss, I have three beautiful royal lobsters, I'll put them down for L'Écailler. At least Gwen will be happy." As I listened to him, I could hear the wind whistling and the sound of the surf against the shore. "I'm going to try the auction in Les Sables-d'Olonne. If the weather is not as bad farther down, I might find sole."

At the same time, an exceptional truffle hunter, Jean Pradel, called me and said, "Damn, the season is over, but I set aside another kilo for you. These are the last ones." This year, I discovered something new with him regarding the aromas of truffles. Jean had me smell three beautiful truffles found on his property, each with a distinct scent. One was herbaceous, another peppery, and the last almost gamey. Noticing my astonished expression, he explained that, similar to wine, the truffle absorbs the characteristics of the weather and the type of soil, taking on different traits based on its terroir. Such moments are well spent. As winter ends, we find ourselves dreaming of spring vegetables. Scallops are nearing their season's end, while both white and green asparagus are beginning to emerge. This is when the price of sole decreases, but that of lamb soars. With Easter approaching, suckling lambs are being prepared for sacrifice. Cows are finally coming out of the barns where they spend their winter, and raw milk is becoming richer, taking on a floral scent. Now is when goat's- and cow's-milk cheeses are at their best.

As we approach May, it's a wonderful time for the markets in the south of France. The vegetable gardens there are flourishing with peas, beans, small artichokes that aspire to become *barigoule* (the Provençal braised artichoke dish), countless lettuces, and vibrant edible flowers. The red fruits are also starting to appear! The first Gariguette strawberries are soaking up the sun. Christophe fills me in with his melodic accent, hoping I overlook the prices.

Meanwhile, nature is slowly awakening in our vegetable garden in Le Perche. Greg, our gardener, is still concerned about the risk of late frost; after three nights at minus four degrees, all the year's hard work could be wiped out. These climatic hazards also affect all our wine-growing friends. On particularly cold nights, hundreds of fires are lit between the rows of vines to create a cushion of warm air, raising the temperature by two or three degrees to protect the tender, developing grape clusters.

Jean Luc, a supplier of Percheron products, walks through the door of the bistro. The conversation is both harsh and friendly. He brought me wonderful products from the region: eggs, a very, very salted butter from the Ferme de l'Étoile, and nearly all of my meat. It's time to talk business. We discuss the nitty-gritty, including quality, quantity, product costs, and origins. The main issue is with the beef tenderloin. I specifically want the Normande breed and more than four kilos. I'm hoping for some concession regarding the price. This conversation is a recurring theme between us; sometimes I come out on top, and sometimes I don't. He seemed particularly confident this morning, making me think I would lose this round. That's just how it is; the most important thing for me is that he remains steadfast on quality rather than compromising for a lower price, so I am the one who often concedes.

When summer comes into full swing, we transition from the vibrant greens of spring to a dazzling array of reds! Strawberries, cherries, blackcurrants, redcurrants, red peppers, eggplants, and peppers fill Greg's crates.

Our vegetable garden is overflowing, and the tomatoes, including Crimean black, Bernese rose, cherry, pineapple, beef heart, and Brandywine, are packed into tight rows. Greg has planted about fifteen varieties, both early and late.

For three months, our menu will feature a salad made with tomatoes from our vegetable garden, seasoned simply with freshly ground pepper, fleur de sel, and a drizzle of Kalamata olive oil delivered by our friend Alex. These outdoor-grown tomatoes, raised without pesticides, have an unmistakable flavor. When some customers choose this salad as an appetizer and again for dessert, we know we have succeeded in our quest for taste and quality. Twice a week, a white van pulls up in front of the bistro with Jean from Maison Borniambuc. He delivers a rich, slightly yellow raw cream (perfect with strawberries), a farmhouse *fromage blanc* with remarkable acidity, and blocks of butter, either salted or unsalted, in which we can savor the taste and aroma of fresh grass or hay, cut according to the season.

There is also my friend Jean-Luc Poujauran, a star baker and absolutely handsome guy who has been providing us with incomparable bread for twenty years. Although we don't see each other often due to our busy schedules, we frequently have long conversations over the phone. During our chats, we love discussing chefs, the latest restaurants that have opened or closed, and, of course, all the different products. To me, Jean-Luc is not just an exceptional baker but also the finest connoisseur of our profession. He has a knack for helping others and is always eager to mentor young chefs.

Following in his footsteps is another talented baker, Benoît Castel. His traditional breads, made from reconstituted flour that includes the previous day's unsold breads, remind me of my childhood. Their smell, satisfying crunch of the crust, and supple texture, which pairs perfectly with fresh butter and red currant jam, bring back fond memories of breakfasts and snacks in the countryside. Just the aroma of freshly sliced bread can brighten my entire day.

The true essence of these impressions unfolds during the annual lunch organized by Benoît at Place Sorbie in the 20th arrondissement, led by our beloved Frédérick E. Grasser-Hermé for the organization l'Amicale du Gras. On this day, the square evokes the spirit of Jacques Tati's *Jour de Fête* (*The Big Day*). Accompanied by the melodies of a player piano, the feast features charcuterie, *pâtés en croûte*, *vol-au-vents*, tarts, and a delightful array of sorbets. The village comes alive with laughter among friends, companions, and amusing characters; nearly everyone in the profession comes together, and the wine flows freely. As summer draws to a close, we still enjoy the last of the tomatoes, but we yearn for comforting hot dishes. We eagerly anticipate the arrival of mushrooms and sizzling parsley butter in the pan, along with tender game birds and furry creatures. It is now the Hebert family's turn to join the festivities. Over the past twenty-five years, we have welcomed the father, mother, son, sister, and now the grandson, all passionate second-hand dealers and dedicated fur traders. Natives of Le Perche, they have no equal when it comes to treating us to mushrooms that include porcini, pied de moutons, chanterelles, delicious milk caps, beefsteaks, and sometimes precious parasols. They arrive late at night like smugglers, and it's as if we are plunged right into the Maurice Genevoix novel *Raboliot*. The mushrooms are neatly arranged in wooden crates covered with ferns. Occasionally, an unlabeled bottle of Calvados is hidden among them, and maybe a pair of pigeons, or even a pretty hare whose unfortunate fate will place it as the centerpiece of *le lièvre à la royale*, a dish served to kings and princes that marks the end of the autumn season.

I cannot leave the beloved Perche without thinking about the mountain of fries we serve daily, which have become a cornerstone of our bistro's reputation. For years, the potatoes for our fries have been delivered to us by the Cotreuil family, who live in a magnificent house in Eperrais. The Cotreuils, descendants of Percherons for three hundred years, are farmers of aristocratic tradition, deeply connected to their region. However, they are perplexed by the modernization of their profession and worried about the future of their land. They feel frustrated by the Parisian newcomers who reject the crowing of roosters, the smell of manure, and the chimes of church bells that ring every quarter hour, day and night. As we slowly transition into winter, it's also time for the hunting season to begin. That's when my friend Rodolphe Paquin from the restaurant Le Repaire de Cartouche steps into the spotlight, as game is his specialty.

Night after night, he walks through the Rungis Market searching for gray partridges, Scottish grouse, and, of course, the famous French hares *en peau* (whole and uncleaned). This Norman giant has always shared his experience and knowledge of the market with me. Often, my phone rings around five o'clock on Tuesday mornings. After a sarcastic exchange of "You were sleeping?" and "Of course I was sleeping!" he tells me about the products he has put together for me. It's a great arrangement—I can enjoy the market without even getting out of bed! That's what friendship is all about. Thanks to him, I've had access to incredible finds at unbeatable prices over the seasons, such as white asparagus or a case of exceptional Caesar's mushrooms, along with a regular supply of game, Sologne strawberries, and other delights.

Some products cross over the seasons. Jean-Yves Bordier and his eponymous Maison, a cheese affineur and manufacturer of a wide range of exceptional butter, have been with us for twenty-five years. Situated in his Breton terroir on the edge of Normandy, the company has married the best of these two regions and their surroundings, for whom they age the best varieties of raw-milk cheeses in their cellars to send to us when they have reached maturity. In this profession, we discover new talents and gems day after day. Once, completely by chance during a conversation at the opening of a photo exhibition, I spotted on a table an imposing piece of aged Salers cheese. As I approached it, the powerful, milky aroma and the thick rind that surrounded it made me feel like I had discovered a treasure. After just two bites in, I was hooked. I had to have this cheese! When I finally uncovered the address where it was produced, I had to fight and beg to finally get my hands on it. Since then, Chantal from La Ferme Auvergnate in Saint-Germain-Lembron has been sending me this marvel of a cheese, accompanied by an utterly addictive Saint-Nectaire.

With Christmas approaching, the excitement builds. There's one more topic to discuss, and it's no less important: Every good meal deserves to be followed by a great cup of coffee, and this was another exceptional encounter. I met an extraordinary person—a vibrant, passionate individual driven by two interests: music and coffee. It was clear he had a true talent for coffee. His small business in Verona, Italy, roasts exceptional coffees for a select group of customers he personally chooses from each country. If you appreciate authentic Italian coffee, you'll recognize the name Gianni Frasi from Giamaica Caffè. His coffee is so unique that as soon as you finish a cup, you insist on another.

DESS

ERTS

GRAND MARNIER SOUFFLÉ

Serves 2

Preparation time: 15 to 20 minutes
Cooking time: 30 minutes

---

2 teaspoons (130 g) unsalted butter
⅓ cup plus 1½ tablespoons (100 ml) whole milk
1 tablespoon (127 g) Grand Marnier
1 large egg yolk
½ cup (100 g) sugar, divided
1 tablespoon plus 2 teaspoons (12 g) cornstarch
2 large egg whites
Pinch salt
Confectioners' sugar, for dusting

1 • Preheat the oven to 350°F (180°C). Grease two 2-inch (5 cm) tall x 4-inch (10 cm) diameter ramekins with the butter.

2 • In a medium saucepan, bring the milk and Grand Marnier to a boil.

3 • In a large bowl, vigorously whisk together the egg yolks, ¼ cup (50 g) of the sugar, and the cornstarch until well combined. Gradually pour the hot milk mixture into the yolk mixture while whisking continuously.

4 • Scrape the entire mixture back into the saucepan and, over medium heat, cook, stirring the whole time, for 1 minute, until a thick pastry cream forms. Remove from the heat and set aside.

5 • In the bowl of a stand mixer fitted with the whisk attachment, beat the egg whites on medium-high speed until they become frothy. Increase the mixer speed to high and sprinkle in the salt and remaining ¼ cup (50 g) sugar. Remove the bowl from the mixing stand and very gently fold the beaten egg whites into the pastry cream.

6 • Divide the soufflé batter evenly between the ramekins, leaving a little space at the top. Bake for 15 to 20 minutes, or until the soufflés have risen about 1 inch (3 cm) above the rims of the ramekins and the tops have turned golden brown. Dust with little confectioners' sugar and serve immediately.

PAUL BERT

MACARONS À LA CHÂTAIGNE

(*Chestnut Macarons*)

lakes about 30 macarons
reparation time: 25 minutes
ooking time: 20 minutes
esting time: 30 minutes

or the Macaron Shells

½ cups (175 g) almond flour
¼ cups (325 g) confectioners' sugar
large (160 g) egg whites, at room temperature
½ tablespoons sugar
inch salt
uice of ½ lemon

or the Chestnut Cream Filling

½ ounces (100 g) unsweetened chestnut puree
cup (250 ml) heavy cream, cold
tablespoons (50 g) sugar

onfectioner's sugar, for dusting
larrons glacé (candied chestnuts), for serving (optional)

• Make the macaron shells: Combine the lmond flour and confectioners' sugar into a ood processor. Run for 30 seconds or until the ngredients have a uniform texture. Sift the almond our and confectioners' sugar mixture into a large owl. In the bowl of a stand mixer fitted with the hisk attachment, beat the egg whites on medium-igh speed until frothy. Add the sugar, salt, and mon juice and beat until the egg whites maintain tiff peaks.

2 • Remove the bowl from the mixing stand. Add the almond flour and confectioners' sugar mixture to the egg whites and combine very gently using a spatula until the batter is smooth.

3 • Preheat the oven to 350°F (180°C).

4 • Scrape the batter into a large pastry bag fitted with a ½-inch (1.25 cm) plain tip and pipe round shells of about 2 inches (5 cm) in diameter on a parchment paper–lined baking sheet. Set the piped shells aside to rest for 30 minutes, then bake for 10 to 15 minutes. The baking temperature may vary slightly from oven to oven, so it is recommended at the end of the baking time to try to peel a shell off the parchment paper. If it comes off easily without sticking, the shells are done. If not, continue baking for several more minutes. Repeat to test their doneness.

5 • Make the chestnut cream filling: In a small bowl, use a spoon to mash the chestnut puree until it is smooth. In the bowl of a stand mixer fitted with the whisk attachment, begin beating the cold cream on medium-high speed. Gradually add the sugar. Add the chestnut puree and beat just until incorporated and thickened, then, using a silicone spatula, fold the mixture until it is creamy smooth and thick enough to pipe. Scrape the filling into a large pastry bag fitted with a large star tip.

6 • Place half the shells flat side up and pipe approximately 1 tablespoon of the filling onto them. Close them with a second shell, pressing down lightly.

7 • Neatly place a macaron on a serving plate and dust with confectioner's sugar and serve with marrons glacé, if desired.

Tip: Throughout the year, we vary the macaron filling according to the season. We also serve them with strawberry, raspberry, and chocolate fillings.

PARIS-BREST

(Choux Pastry Ring with Hazelnut Buttercream Filling)

Makes 6 pastries

Preparation time: 20 minutes
Cooking time: 40-45 minutes
Resting time: 2½ hours

For the Choux Pastry Bases

1 cup (250 ml) water
1 cup (250 ml) whole milk
¾ cup plus 2 tablespoons (1¾ sticks/200 g) unsalted butter
¼ cup (50 g) sugar
1 teaspoon salt
2¼ cups plus 3 tablespoons (300 g) all-purpose flour
7 large (350 g) eggs

For the Buttercream Filling

7 large (140 g) egg yolks
¾ cup (150 g) sugar
¾ cup (100 g) all-purpose flour
1 pound 5 ounces (600 g) unsalted butter
2½ cups (600 ml) whole milk
1 pound 2 ounces (500 g) hazelnut praline paste
Confectioners' sugar
Sliced almonds

---

1 • Make the choux pastry bases: In a large saucepan, bring the water, milk, butter, sugar, and salt to a boil over medium-high heat. Add the flour a little at a time while stirring continuously with a large wooden spoon. When the mixture pulls away from the sides of the pan and resembles a homogenous paste, immediately transfer it to the bowl of a stand mixer fitted with the paddle attachment. Begin beating on medium speed. Add the eggs a little at a time, scraping down the sides and bottom of the bowl as needed. Continue to beat until the mixture is smooth, shiny, and falls slowly from the beater.

2 • Refrigerate for 30 minutes to cool.

3 • Preheat the oven to 350°F (180°C).

4 • Line a baking sheet with a silicone baking mat. Using a pastry bag fitted with a 1½-inch (4 cm) round pastry tube, pipe 6 rings about 6 inches (15 cm) in diameter on top.

5 • Bake for 40 to 45 minutes, or until crisp and golden. Let them cool for 1 hour after removing from the oven.

6 • Make the buttercream filling: Add the egg yolks to a mixing bowl. Add the sugar and mix vigorously using a whisk until the mixture is lightened in color. Add the flour and whisk until smooth.

7 • Cut the butter into small cubes and set aside. In a saucepan, bring the milk to a boil. Add the yolk mixture, then cook for 1 to 2 minutes over medium heat while stirring continuously.

8 • Off the heat, add the butter and whisk vigorously until smooth. Add the praline and whisk vigorously again until incorporated and smooth.

9 • Refrigerate for 1 hour.

10 • Just before serving, cut the choux pastry bases horizontally in half and pipe the buttercream inside using a pastry bag fitted with a medium fluted pastry tube. Garnish with confectioners' sugar and sliced almonds.

PAUL BERT

FIGUES RÔTIES ET GLACE

À LA VANILLE DE TAHITI

(Roasted Figs with Tahitian Vanilla Bean Ice Cream)

Serves 2

Preparation time: 5 minutes
Cooking time: 10 minutes

---

8 medium figs
3½ tablespoons (50 g) unsalted butter
8 teaspoons (40 ml) honey
2 scoops Tahitian vanilla bean ice cream

1 • Preheat the oven to 350°F (180°C).

2 • Rinse the figs under cold running water and thoroughly pat them dry. Remove the stems and score an "x" across the top using a small, sharp knife. Cut the butter into 8 small cubes.

3 • Place the figs in a baking dish. Tuck a cube of butter down into the scored section of each fig, then add 1 teaspoon honey on top of each fig.

4 • Bake for 10 minutes, until softened and cooked through.

5 • Arrange 4 figs on each of 2 serving plates. Serve with a scoop of the ice cream.

Tip: You can also sprinkle a few toasted sliced almonds or a little crumble topping (see page 191) on the figs just before serving to add a textural element.

TARTE TATIN

(Apple Tart)

Makes 1 8-inch (20 cm) tart
Preparation time: 20 minutes
Cooking time: 30 minutes
Resting time: 45 minutes

1 cup (125 g) all-purpose flour
⅛ cup (25 g) sugar plus 6 tablespoons (85 g) for the caramel
Pinch salt
1¾ pounds (¾ kg), about 4 cooking apples
½ cup (1 stick/125 g) unsalted butter, softened plus 5 tablespoons (70 g) for the caramel
Crème fraîche, for serving

1 • In the bowl of a stand mixer fitted with the whisk attachment, combine the flour, ⅛ cup (25 g) of the sugar, and the salt. Switch to the paddle attachment and beat in ½ cup (125 g) butter a little at a time to form a dough. Scrape the dough out onto a sheet of parchment paper and place a second sheet of parchment paper on top. Using a rolling pin, roll out the dough to a circle slightly larger than 8 inches (20 cm), ⅛ inch (3 mm) thick; the dough should have a slightly larger diameter than the pan. Brush off any residual flour. Refrigerate the dough circle for 30 minutes.

2 • Peel the apples. Cut them in half and remove their cores. Cut the apples in half again and set aside.

3 • Preheat the oven to 350°F (180°C).

4 • Make the caramel: In a small, heavy skillet over medium heat, melt together the 6 tablespoons (85 g) sugar and 5 tablespoons (70 g) butter until caramelized, gently swirling the pan a few times. Do not stir and watch it carefully to prevent it from burning. When the caramel is a medium amber color, about 3 minutes, pour it into the bottom of an 8-inch (20 cm) tart pan. If the butter has separated from the caramel, use a whisk to re-homogenize the caramel. Don't worry if there's still some separated butter when you pour the caramel into the pan.

5 • Arrange the apple quarters in a rosette pattern, rounded side down, on top of the caramel. Bake for 15 to 20 minutes, or until the apples have softened and the caramel is bubbling, then let cool at room temperature for about 15 minutes. Meanwhile, increase the oven temperature to 400°F (200°C).

6 • Slide the dough circle on top of the apples and tuck the edges down into the pan. Bake for 10 to 15 minutes, or until the crust is golden. Remove from the oven and allow to cool on a baker's rack for 15 minutes. Invert the tart onto a serving platter while it is still warm. Slice and serve with a little crème fraîche, if desired.

LE BISTROT
UL BERT
Paris

Paris

LE BISTROT
PAUL BERT
Paris

BABA AU RHUM

(Yeast-Raised Cake Soaked in Rum Syrup)

Serves 8

Preparation time: 20 minutes
Cooking time: 30 minutes
Resting time: 1½ hours plus 24 hours

For the Baba Dough

1 teaspoon (8 g) fresh yeast
¼ cup (60 ml) whole milk, at room temperature
1 cup (125 g) all-purpose flour
1 tablespoon sugar
⅓ teaspoon salt
2 tablespoons (30 g) egg (about a half whole egg, yolk and white lightly beaten together, then measured)
3½ tablespoons (50 g) brown butter (see Tip)
1 tablespoon unsalted butter, to grease the molds

For the Syrup

½ orange
½ lime
½ vanilla bean
2 cups (500 ml) water
1¼ cups (250 g) sugar
Scant ½ cup (100 ml) good-quality dark rum

For the Chantilly Cream

⅔ cup (150 ml) heavy cream, cold
1 tablespoon sugar
A few vanilla bean seeds (from about ¼ vanilla bean)

1 • Make the baba dough: In a small bowl, dissolve the yeast in the milk.

2 • In the bowl of a stand mixer fitted with the dough hook, add the flour, sugar, and salt and mix briefly to combine. Add the egg and brown butter, then begin mixing on medium speed. Gradually add the milk-yeast mixture and mix at medium speed to obtain a homogenous dough Scrape down the insides and bottom of the bowl, plus the hook as needed. Beat until the dough gathers up into a soft, cohesive mass around the hook.

3 • Remove the bowl from the stand and cover it with a towel. Set the bowl aside in a warm place, away from drafts, for 1 hour or until doubled.

4 • Roll the dough into 1-ounce (25 g) balls and place into 8 individual greased baba molds about 2¼ inches in diameter by 2¼ inches high (6.5 x 6.5 cm), filling less than halfway. Let rise again in a warm place, away from drafts, until the dough reaches just shy of the tops of the molds, about 45 minutes.

5 • Preheat the oven to 350°F (180°C). Bake the babas for 20 minutes. Immediately unmold and set them aside for 24 hours at room temperature to dry.

6 • Make the syrup: Cut the orange into quarters. Zest the lime into strips. Split the vanilla bean lengthwise in half and scrape out the seeds. In a medium saucepan over high heat, bring the water, sugar, rum, orange, vanilla bean seeds and pods, and lime zest to a boil. Reduce the heat to low heat and cook for 10 minutes, until reduced and slightly syrupy.

7 • Meanwhile, make the Chantilly cream: In the bowl of a stand mixer fitted with the whisk attachment, beat the cold cream, sugar, and vanilla bean seeds on medium-high speed for about 1 minute, until thickened to a dollop consistency.

8 • Place the babas in a high-sided serving dish and pour the hot syrup over them. Serve the babas with extra warm syrup and the Chantilly cream.

Tip: To make brown butter, melt cubes of unsalted butter in a skillet over medium heat, stirring continuously. Remove from the heat after the foam begins to subside, turns a golden brown, and emits a nutty aroma, about 5 minutes.

TARTE FEUILLETÉE AUX FRAISES

CHANTILLY À LA VANILLE

(*Flaky Strawberry Tart, Vanilla Chantilly Cream*)

lakes 1 12-inch (30 cm) tart
reparation time: 20 minutes
ooking time: 25 to 30 minutes

---

ll-purpose flour, for dusting
0½ ounces (300 g) store-bought all-butter puff pastry dough
½ vanilla bean
ust over ¾ cup (200 ml) heavy cream, cold
cup (100 g) confectioners' sugar
0½ ounces (300 g) strawberries
lour

1 • Preheat the oven to 350°F (180°C).

2 • Dust a work surface very lightly with flour. Using a rolling pin, roll out and cut the puff pastry dough into a circle about 12 inches (30 cm) in diameter. Brush off any residual flour. Place the dough circle onto a parchment paper–lined baking sheet and refrigerate to chill for 15 minutes. Using a fork, prick the pastry all over to prevent excessive puffing. Bake for 25 to 30 minutes, or until golden brown. Set onto a baking rack to cool.

3 • Make the Chantilly Cream: Split the vanilla bean lengthwise in half, scrape out the seeds, and set them aside. In the bowl of a stand mixer fitted with the whisk attachment, beat the cold cream, vanilla bean seeds, and ¾ cup (80 g) of the confectioners' sugar on medium-high speed for about 1 minute, until thickened to a dollop consistency.

4 • Rinse the strawberries under cold running water and thoroughly pat them dry with a paper towel. Hull and quarter them into wedges.

5 • Neatly arrange the strawberries on the dough circle. Dust with the remaining confectioners' sugar. Serve with the Chantilly cream on the side.

PAUL BERT

ÎLE FLOTTANTE AUX PRALINES ROSES

(Floating Island [Meringues in Vanilla Custard Sauce] with Pink Pralines)

erves 4 to 6

eparation time: 10 minutes
ooking time: 30 minutes

- **cup (200 g) sugar for the caramel plus 2 tablespoons (25 g) for the meringue plus ¼ cup plus 2½ teaspoons (60 g) for the custard sauce**
- **large (300 g) eggs**
- **inch fine salt**
- **vanilla bean**
- **cups (500 ml) whole milk**
- **½ ounces (100 g) pink pralines**
- **tablespoon sliced almonds**

• Make the caramel: In a small, heavy skillet ver medium heat, melt 1 cup (200 g) of the sugar ntil caramelized, gently swirling the pan a few mes. Do not stir and watch it carefully to prevent from burning. When the caramel is a medium mber color, about 3 minutes, immediately pour e caramel into the bottom of a 10-inch (25.5 cm) ie plate.

• Preheat the oven to 350°F (180°C).

3 • Separate the egg whites and yolks into separate bowls.

4 • Make the meringue: In the bowl of a stand mixer fitted with the whisk attachment, begin beating the egg whites on medium-high speed. Sprinkle in the remaining 2 tablespoons sugar while the egg whites are beating and add the salt. When the meringue holds stiff peaks, transfer it into the pie plate, smoothing it into an even circle on top of the caramel. Bake for 10 minutes or until firm.

5 • Make the custard sauce: Split the vanilla bean lengthwise in half, scrape out the seeds, and set them aside. In a mixing bowl, thoroughly whisk together the yolks and the remaining ¼ cup plus 2½ teaspoons (60 g) sugar. In a medium saucepan, bring the milk and vanilla bean seeds to a boil. As soon as the milk begins to boil, add it a little at a time to the egg-sugar mixture while whisking continuously. Pour the mixture into the saucepan and cook over low heat while stirring continuously until thickened, about 1 to 2 minutes.

6 • Crush the pink pralines with the side of your knife into small pieces.

7 • Strain and divide the custard sauce evenly among 4 to 6 shallow serving bowls. Carefully slice the meringue into wedges, transfer them to the serving bowls, caramel side up, and sprinkle them with the crushed pink pralines and sliced almonds.

FROMAGE BLANC AU COULIS DE FRUITS ROUGES

(Fromage Blanc with Mixed Berry Sauce)

Serves 2

Preparation time: 5 minutes
Cooking time: 30 minutes
Resting time: 1 hour

1¾ ounces (50 g) strawberries
1¾ ounces (50 g) raspberries
1½ tablespoons sugar
Scant 1½ cups (300 g) fromage blanc

1 • Hull the strawberries. Rinse the strawberries and raspberries under a slow stream of cold water and thoroughly pat them dry.

2 • Roughly chop the strawberries and place them in a small saucepan. Add the raspberries and sugar. Cook for 30 minutes over medium heat, stirring regularly, until the berries have broken down. Thoroughly blend them using a food processor or immersion blender. Strain the mixture through a cheesecloth or fine-mesh strainer. Refrigerate for 1 hour to chill completely.

3 • Spoon the fromage blanc into 2 serving cups and spoon the chilled coulis over each one.

JOURNALISTS AND FOOD CRITICS

As you flip through the pages of this book, you will notice that each chapter highlights the names of real individuals who have played varying roles in the creation and evolution of Bistrot Paul Bert. However, we often refrain from disclosing first or last names, as the subject requires greater sensitivity.

In recent years, gastronomy has evolved from a simple craft into a full-fledged industry, complete with its own codes, intermediaries, affiliates, and various media segments, including the press, television, guides, radio shows, and blogs. This landscape is fueled by the new digital economy and social media in which a slew of talented journalists, influencers of all kinds, and bloggers—alongside a few hucksters and not-so-honest individuals—thrive across a world of digital platforms, Instagrammable photo reports, and reality TV shows.

Today, we lowly restaurateurs must navigate this complex jungle of competing demands and temptations.

The relationship between a restaurateur and a journalist can be likened to that of a loving yet antagonistic couple forced to coexist under the same roof. Each party relies on the other: one has something to sell to customers, while the other has stories to share with readers.

In this dynamic, words often clash within a relationship that is not always equitable, intertwining elements of appreciation, independence, secrecy, scheming, compromise, money, and intimacy. However, amid this complexity, there are also moments of friendship, respect, wisdom, and kindness.

Among these journalists are some who are well known, some who believe they are unknown but are recognized as soon as they walk through the door, some who think they still hold influence versus those who genuinely do and cultivate a borderline obsessive discretion, and some who can fill a restaurant with just three sentences.

There are also those who are reluctant to pay and make it obvious, while others insist on covering their entire bill and become annoyed by any attention, viewing it as a compromise. Then there are those who maintain extremely close—some may say incestuous—relationships with chefs that manifest in travel opportunities, accolades, and awards, all cleverly packaged by a host of brands for advertising and commercial purposes. This quid pro quo is integral to a booming industry.

In the more than twenty-five years since we opened, we have experienced fortunate moments when the number of food journalists could be counted on two hands. Their skillfully crafted columns filled our restaurants, their reviews motivated us to improve, and their praise reinforced our choices. Today, however, we must manage our image more carefully. This often involves hiring a "community manager" and posing questions about journalistic ethics and independence. We even sometimes request the right to review future articles, as journalists have increasingly become agents for major brands. But let's be clear: There is nothing illegal or ethically wrong with this new business model; it is a different slant on the same topic and part of the broader commercial evolution of journalism. And as times change, we must also continue to evolve—in ways that stay true to our values.

NAMU

PAUL BERT

CRÈME CARAMEL

Serves 4

Preparation time: 10 minutes
Cooking time: 45 minutes plus 10 minutes (caramel)
Resting time: 8 hours

- **¼ cup plus 2 tablespoons (80 g) sugar for the caramel plus ½ cup (100 g) for the custard**
- **2 cups (500 ml) whole milk**
- **½ vanilla bean, cut in half lengthwise**
- **3 large (150 g) eggs**

1 • Preheat the oven to 350°F (180°C). Have ready 4 individual 6-ounce (180-ml) custard cups measuring about 2½ to 3 inches (6 to 8 cm) in diameter.

2 • Make the caramel: In a heavy-bottom saucepan over medium heat, melt ¼ cup plus 2 tablespoons (80 g) of the sugar until caramelized, gently swirling the pan a few times. Do not stir and watch it carefully to prevent it from burning. When the caramel is a dark amber color, 5 to 10 minutes, immediately remove it from the heat. Divide the caramel among the custard cups, swirling them to fully coat the bottoms.

3 • Make the custard base: Pour the milk into a small saucepan, scrape the seeds from the vanilla bean, add them to the milk, and bring to a boil. Set it aside off the heat.

4 • In a large bowl, thoroughly whisk together the eggs and the remaining ½ cup (100 g) sugar until the mixture lightens in color to a pale yellow. Add the warm milk a little at a time to the egg-sugar mixture while whisking continuously.

5 • Strain the custard into a bowl (preferably one with a spout). Divide the custard among the cups on top of the caramel. Place the cups in a baking dish and fill it with very hot water halfway up the cups. Bake for 45 minutes, or until just set.

6 • Remove the cups from the water bath to a wire rack and cool for 30 minutes.

7 • Cover each cup with plastic wrap and refrigerate for at least 8 hours.

8 • To serve, run a small knife around the top edge of each cup to loosen the custard. Place a small plate on top of the cup and invert to release the custard with the caramel at the bottom pouring over the custard and pooling on the plate.

Clos des Corvées
2008
Beaune-Villages
ARBOIS PUPILLIN
Maison Pierre OVERNOY
HOUILLON - OVERNOY

ARBOIS PUPILLIN
Maison Pierre OVERNOY
Mis en bouteille par
Gaec HOUILLON - OVERNOY
Sebastien
DOMAINE DE LA CHAPPE VINCENT THOMAS
VIN DE FRANCE
Vin de France

CANNELÉS

Makes about 60 mini cannelés

Preparation time: 10 minutes
Cooking time: 1 hour
Resting time: 8 hours

---

3 cups (750 ml) whole milk
½ cup (1 stick/120 g) unsalted butter
½ vanilla bean
3 large (150 g) eggs
3 large (60 g) egg yolks
1¾ cups plus 2 tablespoons (375 g) sugar
1¼ cups (150 g) all-purpose flour
¼ cup (60 ml) dark rum

1 • In a medium saucepan, bring the milk to a boil. Set aside off the heat.

2 • In a small skillet, heat the butter until melted and lightly browned. Set aside off the heat.

3 • Split the vanilla bean in half lengthwise and scrape out the seeds. In a large mixing bowl, combine the eggs, egg yolks, sugar, flour, and vanilla bean seeds. Vigorously whisk until smooth. Add the warm milk while whisking vigorously.

4 • Strain the mixture. Add the rum and brown butter and whisk vigorously until the batter is smooth.

5 • Refrigerate for 8 hours.

6 • Preheat the oven to 350°F (180°C).

7 • Divide the batter among approximately 20 mini ungreased metal or copper cannelé molds about 1½ inches (4.5 cm) in diameter (it is very important not to use silicone), leaving a little space at the top of each mold. Bake for 1 hour, until the tops are a dark brown.

8 • Set aside for several minutes to cool slightly, to prevent burning your hands, then unmold.

BISTROT
BERT

PAUL

PROFITEROLES

(Choux Puffs with Ice Cream and Chocolate Sauce)

Makes about 40 choux puffs

Preparation time: 10 minutes
Cooking time: 35 minutes
Resting time: 1½ hours

---

1 cup (250 ml) water
1 cup (250 ml) whole milk
¾ cup plus 2 tablespoons (1¾ sticks/200 g) unsalted butter
¼ cup (50 g) sugar
1 teaspoon salt
2¼ cups plus 3 tablespoons (300 g) all-purpose flour
7 large (350 g) eggs
2½ cups (600 ml) vanilla ice cream
Sliced almonds

For the Chocolate Sauce

6½ ounces (185 g) dark chocolate
1½ cups (300 ml) heavy cream

1 • In a large saucepan, bring the water, milk, butter, sugar, and salt to a boil on medium-high heat. Add the flour a little at a time while stirring continuously with a large wooden spoon. When the mixture comes away from the sides of the pan and resembles a homogenous paste, immediately transfer it to the bowl of a stand mixer fitted with the paddle attachment. Begin beating on medium speed. Add the eggs a little at a time, scraping down the sides and bottom of the bowl as needed. Beat until the mixture is smooth.

2 • Refrigerate the dough for 30 minutes.

3 • Preheat the oven to 350°F (180°C).

4 • Line a baking sheet with a silicone baking mat. Using a pastry bag fitted with a 1½-inch (4 cm) round pastry tube, pipe 40 uniform mounds on top, about 2 inches (5 cm) in diameter.

5 • Bake for 40 to 45 minutes, or until crisp and golden. Set aside for 1 hour to cool.

6 • Make the chocolate sauce: Gently melt the chocolate over a double boiler. When the chocolate is completely melted, add the cream and stir vigorously to combine. Set aside.

7 • Cut the choux puffs horizontally in half and place a scoop of vanilla ice cream in each one, then replace the tops. Arrange the filled puffs on serving plates. Pour the melted chocolate and sprinkle the sliced almonds over the top before serving immediately.

Tip: It is difficult to make this recipe for a small quantity of puffs. Freeze any unused ones and thaw them as you need them.

PAVLOVA AUX FRUITS ROUGES

(Baked Meringue with Mixed Berries)

Serves 8 to 10

Preparation time: 20 minutes
Cooking time: 1 hour
Resting time: 45 minutes

---

6 large (180 g) egg whites, at room temperature
1¼ cups (250 g) sugar plus 1 tablespoon for the Chantilly cream
1 teaspoon white vinegar
2 teaspoons cornstarch
1 cup (240 ml) heavy cream, cold
5¼ ounces (150 g) strawberries
5¼ ounces (150 g) raspberries

---

1 • In the bowl of a stand mixer fitted with the whisk attachment, begin beating the egg whites on medium-high speed. With the mixer running, slowly sprinkle in the 1¼ cups (250 g) of the sugar, 1 tablespoon at a time. When all the sugar has been added, turn off the mixer and add the white vinegar. Whisk for 10 seconds, then sift in the cornstarch. Whisk on high for 20 seconds to blend. Continue whisking on high until the meringue holds stiff peaks. Scrape the meringue into a very large pastry bag fitted with a 1½-inch (4 cm) round pastry tube. Alternatively, transfer the meringue to the prepared baking sheet with a large spoon, creating decorative peaks with the spoon back.

2 • Preheat the oven to 245°F (120°C).

3 • Line a baking sheet with parchment paper and pipe the meringue onto the baking sheet into a disk about 10 inches (25 cm) in diameter and about 1 to 1½ inches (3 to 4 cm) thick. Bake for 60 to 80 minutes, or until the shell is firm on the outside.

4 • Let the meringue cool completely in the oven, about 1 hour, before completing the dessert.

5 • Make the Chantilly Cream: In the bowl of a stand mixer fitted with the whisk attachment, beat the cold cream and the remaining 1 tablespoon sugar on medium-high speed for about 1 minute, or until it holds medium-soft peaks and thickens to a dollop consistency.

6 • Rinse the strawberries and raspberries under a slow stream of cold water and thoroughly pat them dry. Hull and quarter the strawberries.

7 • Spoon the Chantilly cream on top of the meringue disk and neatly arrange the berries on top. Serve.

FRAISES ET CRÈME CRUE ENTIÈRE

(*Strawberries and Crème Fraîche*)

Serves 2

Preparation time: 5 minutes

10½ ounces (300 g) strawberries
Confectioners' sugar, for dusting
Scant ½ cup (100 g) crème fraîche

1 • Hull the strawberries and trim their bases a little. Rinse the strawberries under cold water. Thoroughly pat them dry.

2 • Arrange the strawberries on 2 serving plates. Dust with confectioners' sugar. Place a quenelle of crème fraîche on the side of each.

ANANAS RÔTI BEURRE AU RHUM

ET GLACE À LA VANILLE DE TAHITI

(Roasted Pineapple, Rum Butter, and Tahitian Vanilla Bean Ice Cream)

Serves 2

Preparation time: 5 minutes
Cooking time: 6 to 7 minutes

---

2 thick slices very ripe pineapple
2 tablespoons turbinado sugar
2 tablespoons unsalted butter
2 tablespoons dark rum
2 scoops Tahitian vanilla bean ice cream

1 • In a large heavy skillet over medium heat, melt the sugar until caramelized, gently swirling the pan a few times. Do not stir and watch it carefully to prevent it from burning. When the caramel is a medium amber color, about 2 to 3 minutes, add the butter and rum, then add the pineapple slices.

2 • Cook for 2 or 3 minutes while continuously spooning the caramel sauce from the pan over the pineapples, until softened and starting to brown in spots.

3 • Serve the slices with a little of the cooking juices over the top and a scoop of the ice cream.

BISTROT
PAUL BERT

LE BISTROT
PAUL BERT

CRÊPES SUZETTE

(Flambéed Crêpes in Orange Sauce)

Serves 2 to 4 (about 8 crêpes total)

Preparation time: 10 minutes
Cooking time: 20 minutes plus 6 to 7 minutes (sauce)

For the Orange Sauce

1 organic orange
2 teaspoons sugar
1 cup (250 ml) orange juice
2 tablespoons unsalted butter
4 tablespoons Grand Marnier orange liqueur

For the Crêpe Batter

1 cup (250 ml) whole milk
2 tablespoons brown butter (see Tip, page 238)
2 large (100 g) eggs
2 tablespoons sugar
¼ teaspoon salt
1 cup (125 g) all-purpose flour
Neutral-flavor oil

1 • Make the orange sauce: Rinse the orange under cold running water. In a small saucepan, combine the sugar, orange juice, and butter. Zest one quarter of the orange into the pan. Cook over medium-high heat for about 10 minutes, or until the liquid is reduced to approximately ½ cup. Set aside and keep warm.

2 • Make the crêpe batter: In a large bowl, whisk together the milk, brown butter, eggs, sugar, and salt. Add the flour a little at a time while whisking to combine.

3 • Grease a 10-inch (25.5-cm) crêpe pan with the neutral oil using a lightly greased paper towel and preheat over medium heat. Ladle approximately 3 to 4 tablespoons of the batter into the center of the pan, tilting it to spread the batter evenly. Cook for about 1 minute on each side, or until the crêpe is just starting to brown in spots and curl at the edges. Repeat with the remaining batter. Grease the pan again in the same way after each crêpe is completed. Place the finished crêpes on a plate and keep them warm in a low oven.

4 • Fold 4 warm crêpes into quarters and return them to the pan. Alternatively, you can arrange 4 warm crêpes on 2 flame-proof serving dishes. Cover them with the warm sauce and 2 tablespoons each of the Grand Marnier. Light with a long match to flambé, then serve.

LE FONDANT AU CHOCOLAT DE MA GRAND-MÈRE

ET SA CRÈME ANGLAISE

(My Grandmother's Chocolate Cake with Vanilla Custard Sauce)

Makes 1 8-inch (20 cm) round cake (Serves 8)

Preparation time: 10 minutes
Cooking time: 1 hour

For the Chocolate Cake

1 tablespoon unsalted butter, for greasing the pan plus ¾ cup plus 2 tablespoons (1¾ sticks/200 g)

2 (3.5-ounce/100 g) dark chocolate bars, chopped into even pieces

4 large (200 g) eggs

1¼ cups (250 g) sugar

For the Custard Sauce

12 large (240 g) egg yolks

¼ cup (30 g) sugar

1 vanilla bean

4 cups (1 L) whole milk

Confectioners' sugar, for dusting

1 • Preheat the oven to 350°F (180°C).

2 • Line the bottom of an 8-inch (20 cm) round cake pan with a round piece of parchment paper cut to the same diameter as the pan. Generously grease the parchment and sides of the pan with butter.

3 • Make the chocolate cake: In a medium saucepan over medium heat, heat ¾ cup plus 2 tablespoons (1¾ sticks/200 g) of the butter until melted and lightly browned. Turn off the heat, add the chocolate, and let melt. Stir to combine and let cool briefly while you prepare the eggs.

4 • In a large bowl, vigorously whisk together the eggs and sugar.

5 • Slowly scrape the chocolate and butter mixture into the egg-sugar mixture, whisking vigorously until smooth.

6 • Scrape the batter into the pan and bake for 40 minutes, or until set but still very moist.

7 • Meanwhile, make the custard sauce: In a medium bowl, thoroughly whisk together the egg yolks and sugar. Split the vanilla bean lengthwise in half and scrape out the seeds. In a small saucepan, bring the milk and vanilla bean seeds to a boil. As soon as the milk begins to boil, slowly pour it into the yolk-sugar mixture a little at a time while whisking continuously. When all the milk has been added, scrape the mixture into the saucepan. Set over low heat and cook while stirring continuously until thickened to a sauce consistency, about 10 minutes.

8 • Spoon the custard sauce into 2 shallow serving plates and place a slice of the cake on top. Dust with confectioners' sugar and serve.

LE BISTROT
PAUL BERT
LE BISTROT
PAUL BERT

TRADE
PRODUCE OF FRANCE
A. AUBOYNEAU & FILS
70 CLS.
COGNAC
Le COGNAC AUBOYNEAU est le produit
récoltés et distillés dans la région
telle qu'elle est délimitée par le décret du

CHURROS ET SAUCE AU CHOCOLAT

(Churros and Chocolate Sauce)

Serves 3

Preparation time: 10 minutes
Cooking time: 25 minutes
Resting time: 1 hour

For the Chocolate Sauce

2⅛ ounces (60 g) dark chocolate
Scant ½ cup (100 ml) heavy cream

For the Churro Batter

1 cup (250 ml) water
¼ cup (56 g) unsalted butter
1 tablespoon (13 g) sugar
½ teaspoon salt
1 cup (125 g) all-purpose flour
1 large egg, beaten

For frying and serving

Neutral-flavor oil, for deep frying
Confectioners' sugar, for dusting

1 • Make the chocolate sauce: Gently melt the chocolate over a double boiler. When the chocolate is completely melted, add the cream and stir vigorously to combine. Set aside.

2 • Make the churro batter: In a large saucepan, combine 1 cup (250 ml) water, butter, sugar, and salt. Over medium heat, bring the mixture to a simmer. Add all the flour into the liquid mixture in the pan and, using a wooden spoon, stir until the dough is smooth and well incorporated. The texture should be firm but pliable. Scrape the dough into a mixing bowl fitted with the paddle attachment and allow to cool for 5 minutes.

3 • With the mixer running at medium speed, add the beaten egg. Beat until the mixture comes together and is smooth. Scrape the warm churro dough into a large pastry bag fitted with a fluted pastry tube measuring about ⅝ inch (1.5 cm) in diameter.

4 • Fry the churros: Preheat a deep fryer or large heavy pot with at least 1 inch (2.5 cm) of oil to 360°F (180°C).

5 • Pipe and cut the batter into portions measuring about 4 inches (10 cm) long above the hot oil, allowing them to fall into the oil as you cut them one after the other. Cook each portion (about 12 total) for about 2 to 3 minutes, or until golden brown. Remove the churros from the hot oil with a slotted spoon and place them on a paper towel–lined plate to absorb as much oil as possible. Continue with the remaining batter.

6 • To serve: Sprinkle with the confectioners' sugar and serve with the chocolate sauce on the side for dipping.

PAUL BERT

RIZ AU LAIT

(Rice Pudding)

Serves 2

Preparation time: about 20 minutes
Resting time: 2 hours 45 minutes

½ vanilla bean
Just over ¾ cup (200 ml) whole milk
1½ tablespoons sugar
⅔ cup (120 g) short-grain rice
1 tablespoon unsalted butter

1 • Split the vanilla bean lengthwise in half and scrape out the seeds. Add the seeds and pod to the milk. Refrigerate for 2 hours to infuse.

2 • In a medium saucepan over medium heat, bring the infused milk (still containing the vanilla bean) to a boil. Reduce the heat to low and add the sugar and rice to the hot milk and stir to combine. Cook uncovered over low heat for about 20 minutes, or until the rice is tender. Stir every few minutes during the cooking time to prevent sticking.

3 • At the end of the cooking time, remove the vanilla bean. Add the butter and stir to combine. Pour the mixture into a serving dish and let cool for 45 minutes at room temperature before serving.

SOUPE AU CHOCOLAT NOIR

(Dark Chocolate Soup)

Serves 2

Preparation time: 5 minutes
Cooking time: 10 minutes
Resting time: 1 hour 20 minutes

¼ large (5 g) egg yolk
¼ cup (50 g) sugar
7 ounces (200 g) dark chocolate (75 to 80% cacao)
1 cup (250 ml) whole milk
1 cup (250 ml) heavy cream

1 • In a medium bowl, vigorously whisk together the egg yolk and sugar. Set aside.

2 • Roughly chop the chocolate and set aside.

3 • In a medium saucepan over medium heat, bring the milk and cream to a boil. Reduce the heat to low and whisk in the yolk-sugar mixture. Cook for about 10 minutes, whisking continuously, then strain into a bowl. The mixture should be steaming hot and only very slightly reduced.

4 • Add the chocolate pieces to the hot mixture. Stir until the chocolate is completely melted. Let cool at room temperature for about 20 minutes, then blend using an immersion blender until smooth. Refrigerate for 1 hour. Serve.

JACQUES TATI
Play Time
LE TEMPS DES LOISIRS
CHAUFFAGE
utilisez
LE
FRAGILE
LES HUITRES
CADORET

BONBONS
PARFUMÉS
MANTALO

LE BISTROT
PAUL BERT
Paris
18 RUE PAUL BERT, 75011

Bistrot
Paul Bert

BISTROT PAUL BERT
A la carte
TERRINE DE CAMPAGNE MAISON
CARPACCIO DE BOEUF AU BASILIC
CARPACCIO DE DAURADE
SALADE DE TOMATES MULTICOLORES AU BASILIC
SOLE MEUNIÈRE
POMMES VAPEUR
TARTARE DE BOEUF, FRITES MAISON & SALADE VERTE
ROGNON DE VEAU À LA MOUTARDE, PURÉE MAISON
CARRÉ D'AGNEAU RÔTI AU JUS, PETITS POIS, CAROTTES
ASSIETTE DE FROMAGES
CRÈME CARAMEL
ÎLE FLOTTANTE AUX PRALINES ROSES
TARTE FINE AUX POMMES
SOUFFLÉ GRAND MARNIER
MACARON AUX FRAISES
CRÈME CRUE
15€

ACKNOWLEDGMENTS

To Gwen, without whom this adventure never would have happened.

To my children Corentine and Benjamin, whose strollers were in our bistros for a long time, and who later accepted our daily and often nightly absences with stoicism—I hope they don't hold it against us too much.

To my son Thomas, who is passionate about cooking, who worked with us, and who passed on to us magnificent recipes learned at Gérard Besson's—such as Hare à la Royale and Paris-Brest—before flying off to the Land of the Rising Sun, where he settled.

To my eldest son, Patrick, who always met the changes in my life with a smile and whose insights often proved to be correct.

To Anne Marie and Jacques Cadoret who, after careful consideration, let me love their daughter, and who gave me a family.

To Sébastien Alessandri, my friend and partner at the very beginning, who didn't have time to make it official.

To Michel Picard, who taught me everything about this profession, which I knew nothing about before meeting him, and whose presence I have missed every day for eighteen years.

To Sébastien Demorand, whose phenomenal sense of culture, knowledge of our profession, and brilliant invention of the word "Bistronomy"—a mashup of "bistro" and "gastronomy"—inspired countless late-night conversations that helped us define the ethos and the limitations of our bistros, sometimes aided by glasses half-full and, too often, half-empty.

To Thierry, our chef of twenty-five years, who runs the kitchen with a firm hand and who has accepted all my culinary eccentricities.

To my journalist friends François Simon, Jean-Claude Ribaut, and many others, who have offered us unfailing support through the years, and who have often been the safeguards of our reputation, encouraging us to keep cool heads amidst rapid change and boosting our morale when the boat was rocking.

To Wendy Lyn, an American who whispers in the ears of chefs from Paris to New York, via Venice, and who is clearly to thank for our popularity in the US. I cannot count the number of amazing chefs and American clients who have come to us through her, from Anthony Bourdain to Andrew Zimmerman.

To Yves Camdeborde, who wrote such a beautiful preface for this book and whose friendship is a treasure.

To Rodolphe Paquin, of Le Repaire de Cartouche, who is my friend first and foremost, and who is also a wonderful cook and a joyful table companion. We have shared many bottles together, and I take great pride in knowing that I have helped him learn to love the ocean.

To all the winemakers who have taught me to love natural wine. It's impossible to name them all—an entire chapter wouldn't be enough—but I have great affection for Domaine Gramenon, whose cuvées La Mémé and A Pascal S were an incredible revelation—thank you, Michèle! Jean Foillard's Morgon and later Eric Pfifferling's Tavel knocked me off my feet. Of course, the wines from the Arena family, which carry on the legacy of Antoine, the godfather of all natural winemakers. Right on brand for a Corsican! Jokes aside, they are my friends above all else; I like to say, "If I die, don't forget to put their bottles in the box." Until then, I much prefer to drink them with all of you, as I dream of the 2045 vintage....

To Patricia Brandt and her husband, American friends who are in love with France, its culture, and its cuisine; they spend a month in Paris every year, always reserving table 8 at 8 p.m. for the four Fridays of their stay, as they have been doing for many years.

To Annabelle Schachmes, the whirlwind photographer and attentive scribe. Hers are the hidden hands behind this book.

To all the people who have passed through the dining room and kitchen, some for a few days, others for months or years, who have helped fill these bistros with the energy and friendliness that mark our proud reputation.

INDEX

For Abrams:
Editor: Laura Dozier
Design Manager: Darilyn Lowe Carnes
Managing Editor: Amy Vinchesi
Production Manager: Larry Pekarek
Translated from the French by Zachary R. Townsend

For Hachette Livre:
Managing director and publisher: Catherine Saunier-Talec
Photographs pages 172–173: © Yves Duronsoy
Managing Editor: Lisa Grall
Editor: Jeanne Mauboussin-Ledoux
Art Director: Nicolas Gallois
Layout: Cécile Rabataud
Typsetting: Mélanie Rébillaud
Proofreading: Marie-Eve Foutiau
Production: Amélie Latsch
Partnership Manager: Dana Lichiardopol (dlichiardopol@hachette-livre.fr)

Library of Congress Control Number: 2025933183

ISBN: 978-1-4197-8400-2
eISBN: 979-8-88707-848-9

First published in France under the title: *Le Paul Bert: Les Recettes Cultes D'un Vrai Bistrot Parisien*

Printed and bound in China
10 9 8 7 6 5 4 3 2 1

ABRAMS The Art of Books
195 Broadway, New York, NY 10007
abramsbooks.com

ABRAMS is represented in the UK and Europe by Abrams & Chronicle Books, 1 West Smithfield, London EC1A 9JU and Média-Participations, 57 rue Gaston Tessier, 75166 Paris, France.
www.abramsandchronicle.co.uk and www.media-participations.com

info@abramsandchronicle.co.uk

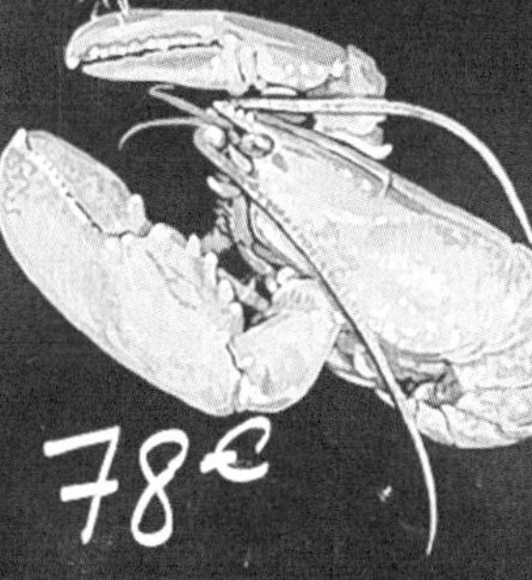
MENU
HOMARD
78€
12 Huîtres plates du Belon n°5
½ HOMARD BLEU AU KARI-GOSSE
ET SES FRITES MAISON
Emincé de pommes, caramel
au beurre salé; glace vanille
T.T.C. S.C.

LE PAUL BERT à la carte